Shpil

The Art of Playing Klezmer

Edited by Yale Strom

THE SCARECROW PRESS, INC.
Lanham • Toronto • Plymouth, UK
2012

Published by Scarecrow Press, Inc.
A wholly owned subsidary of The Rowman & Littlefield Publishing Group, Inc.
4501 Forbes Boulevard, Suite 200, Lanham, Maryland 20706
www.rowman.com

10 Thornbury Road, Plymouth PL6 7PP, United Kingdom

British Library Cataloguing in Publication Information Available

Library of Congress Cataloging-in-Publication Data
Shpil : the art of playing klezmer / edited by Yale Strom.
      pages cm
  Includes bibliographical references and index.
  ISBN 978-0-8108-8291-1 (pbk. : alk. paper) — ISBN 978-0-8108-8292-8 (ebook)
  1. Klezmer music—History and criticism.   2. Songs, Yiddish—History and criticism.
3. Jews—Music—History and criticism.   I. Strom, Yale.
  ML3528.8.S53 2012
  781.62'924—dc23   2012022715

Printed in the United States of America.

Contents

Note on the Transliteration of Yiddish Text

As with any foreign language that does not use the Latin alphabet, Yiddish has often been spelled the way users deem closest to its sound. For example, Poles might write *sznajder* (tailor) while Americans, relying on the German spelling, would write *schneider*. There are many spelling land mines in Yiddish because the language is derived from several others (German, Hebrew, Polish, Russian, and French), all of which are in use today. There are even spelling discrepancies for Yiddish words that have crossed into English. For example, the word *Chanuka*, originally a Hebrew word, can be spelled *Chanukah*, *Hanukah*, or *Hanukkah*. But according to the academic guidelines set up by the YIVO Institute (Yiddish Scientific Institute), the Yiddish word for the Festival of Lights is spelled *Khanike*.

Since this is a book about klezmer music and the Jewish world in Eastern Europe, where Yiddish was for the most part the lingua franca among all Jewish musicians and their Jewish neighbors (even Jewish immigrants who came to New York City), all the Yiddish and Hebrew words in this book are spelled according to the YIVO standard—even those in everyday English usage.

Preface

Yale Strom

In 1981, I embarked on my journey to discover the essence of my East European Jewish heritage. Little did I know that the art and culture of the Jewish folk musician, the klezmer, would become one of my lifelong passions. Years later, I realized I was following in the footsteps of the great Jewish ethnographer S. Ansky (Shloyme Zanvl Rappoport, 1863–1920), exactly eighty years after he began his ethnographic trek through the Czarist lands of Poland, Lithuania, Belarus, and Ukraine searching for anything do to with Jewish culture—including klezmer music. This folk music had been heard throughout Central and Eastern Europe for nearly a thousand years, but in less than six years the haunting sonorous sounds of the klezmer had been all but silenced as a result of the Holocaust. But had it completely vanished? Was there not a single person who could play me a *freylekhs* or a *khusidl*? Could no one remember what transpired at a Jewish wedding when the musicians began to play? Armed with the Jewish upbringing my parents generously provided and youthful gumption, my yearlong sojourn in the former Eastern Bloc brought me in contact with many Jewish and Roma informants who played klezmer or remembered hearing the music at a Jewish wedding or some other kind of celebration where they were playing. And thus my education about klezmer music and culture began.

Zoltan Kodály (1882–1967), the superb Hungarian composer, performer, ethnomusicologist, and music educator, believed that everyone had two mother tongues: the language spoken at home and their folk music. For the Jews of Eastern Europe, Yiddish was the language of the mind, while klezmer music and Yiddish folk songs were languages of the heart. Without klezmer musicians, many customs pertaining to weddings and other celebratory events and the language to describe them would never have existed.

Albert Einstein said that "the only source of knowledge is experience." All the contributors to this book have had many years of practical experience. To experience klezmer music through listening or playing will give you a keen insight into Eastern European Jewish culture. Whether you are a professional or an amateur musician, I hope you will receive the same hours of pleasure I have from learning and playing klezmer. I invite you to join me on the journey.

Acknowledgments

I would like to thank my parents, Norman and Sandi Licht, for their support and encouragement and for buying my first drum kit for my *bar mitsve*. I'd also like to thank Yale Evelev (Luaka Bop) for giving me Frank London's telephone number the first week I moved to New York City in 1985 and Henry Sapoznik for introducing me to Pete Sokolow. Finally, a special thanks to my dear wife, Karen Heifetz, who put up with my touring and shenanigans for more than twenty-four years and has done more than her share helping raise our wonderful kids, Jacob and Bess.

—David Licht

I would like to thank many people who have figured in the story of my forty-year career in music, but only some can be mentioned here. My contrabass teachers, Federico Silva and Bertram Turetzky, taught not only principles of music but also the meaning of making art and respect for tradition. Lifelong friends (and musicians) Fred Benedetti and Yale Strom have provided encouragement and example through their achievements. My wife, Beatriz (who was in the original Buenos Aires cast of *Hair*), introduced me to the world of dance and dance music in general. Irish guitarist and recording engineer Brian Baynes, recording engineer Darrell Harvey, musical theater producer John Moores Jr., and audio producer Peter Dyson have all been among the most gracious in informing and furthering my career.

—Jeff Pekarek

I would like to give thanks to those who have always supported my singing, including Hanna Griff of the Eldridge Street Museum (who invited me to make history); my father for his voice and my mother for the constant piano music, both of which filled my childhood; my friends and teachers; and most especially my wonderful bandmates, who have always backed me up—both literally and figuratively. Last but not at all least, my love and thanks to Yale Strom: my partner, teacher, and best friend; and Tallulah Strom, who gives me a reason to sing.

—Elizabeth Schwartz

I would like to thank my father, Felix, for introducing me to the soul and sound of Jewish music from the source and my mother, Luba, for supporting my musical endeavors and for taking me to hear the *klezmorim* when they started back in 1975. To my brother Richard, for sparking and encouraging my serious musical development, my grandmother Raschele Bakst for passing on the emotional sentiment of the Jewish soul to me, and all of my family members who perished in the Holocaust. To Lev Liberman and David Julian Gray (original reed players of the klezmorim) for inspiring me and showing me how it's done, Ben Goldberg for sharing his knowledge, and three very important music teachers who guided and helped me hone my skills: Wyatt Kirth (junior high), Alan Close (high school), and Joe Thompson (summer school). Lastly but certainly not least, my wife, Karen, who helped me develop a beautiful flute tone, and for her strength and support throughout the years.

—Norbert Stachel

I would like to first thank my father for giving me the initial opportunity to learn the accordion, inspiring me to go to music school, and making music an important part of our family heritage. I would like to thank my music teacher, Harold Seletsky, who gave me the first opportunity to play klezmer in his ensemble West Side Klezmorim. He taught me much about music and even more about life. To all the great musicians whom I have had the pleasure of performing with, particularly Yale Strom & Hot Pstromi; they allowed and encouraged me to bring my own musical personality to my interpretation of klezmer. Our travels around the world made us close personally, and that came out in the music. Lastly, I want to thank my dear Roma friend and musician Zoran Muncan, who inspired me with his musicianship and constructive criticism of me.

—Peter Stan

I would like to thank my mother for passing on her love of art and quality of perseverance, my father for his love of Jewish culture, Mrs. Baker of Detroit who gave me my first violin lessons at Vernor Elementary School, my siblings who put up with many hours of violin practicing, and especially all my bandmates who have helped me become a better musician and person. I am also indebted to all the Jewish and Roma informants I met over the years in Eastern Europe who gave me vital information about klezmer music. Last but most importantly my respect, admiration, and love for my artistic collaborator and wife, Elizabeth Schwartz, and to my effervescent daughter, Tallulah, who shares my love of music and running.

—Yale Strom

1

A History of Klezmer from the Middle Ages to the Twentieth Century

Yale Strom

Music has been a vital part of Jewish culture since biblical times. The first Jewish musician mentioned in the Bible is Jubal, son of Lamech, who played the harp and organ. In ancient Israel, there were Jews, who played secular music in their daily lives, and the Levites, who were specifically trained to perform only sacred music in the temple. The ancient Jews, like their neighbors, believed that music held magical powers and could inspire the performer and listener to great spiritual ecstasy, and could even help to foretell the future and treat mental illness. "Whenever the evil spirit of God came upon Saul, David would take the lyre and play it; Saul would find relief and feel better, and the evil spirit would leave him."[1]

After the destruction of the Second Temple in 70 CE, the Jews were dispersed throughout the world, and the Levites' sacred temple services were no longer needed. The rabbis then banned all instrumental music with the explanation that their congregants should be in mourning for Zion. This self-imposed mourning was to be lifted only once the Messiah came to rebuild the temple. The rabbis associated any kind of secular music with the decadence of Greek culture. "It became synonymous with obscenity and was chiefly used for carnal purposes at frivolous occasions. No wonder, then, that Judaism opposed profane music."[2]

Unfortunately, these extreme attitudes held by many rabbis from the beginning of the common era through the seventeenth century created a negative social attitude among the Jewish community toward the klezmer.[3]

In the Christian Middle Ages, secular music and song were represented by wandering troubadours, minstrels, minnesingers,[4] *shpielleutter*,[5] and jongleurs[6] who entertained both at the courts of the aristocracy and in market squares across Europe. Jews participated in this art form as well and were called *shpilman*.[7] As a result of the rabbi's disapproval (and because synagogues and private homes were becoming too small), Jews built their own dance halls.

These dance halls, known as *Juden Spielhaus* in German (where people also played cards and watched theater), became a fixture in many of the Jewish ghettos of Germany, France, Holland, and Switzerland. Jewish itinerant musicians would perform in these dance halls. One of the earliest known Jewish dance halls was in Augsburg, Germany, in 1190.[8] And in Frankfurt am Main in 1390, a guild of Jewish musicians was hired to play at both Jewish and gentile dance halls for weekly dances.[9] As the popularity of the Jewish dance hall continued to grow, rabbis were forced to relax their ineffective prohibitions against women singing in public, playing instrumental music, and dancing with men.

About one hundred years before the existence of Jewish dance halls, the itinerant Jewish shpilman was generally a musician. But as these wandering musicians began to incorporate other light and serious forms of entertainment (such as being clowns), German Jews began to refer to them as *letsim* (pl.),[10] *possenreiser* (pl.),[11] and sometimes even as *narim* (pl.).[12] Over time the profession of the *lets* evolved into that of the *marshalik*[13] and *batkhn*.[14] To complicate matters, these names were sometimes interchangeable for lets. From written evidence, it appears that these various occupations gradually melded into that of the klezmer (a term popular from the eighteenth century through today).

Jewish musicians from the Middle Ages through the seventeenth century in Germany, Bohemia, Moravia, and Silesia played a variety of instruments, including the cittern, lute, zither, shawm, harp, flageolet and harpsichord, *dudelzak*, *Judenleier*, *positive*, *Judenharfe*, *zink*, and *hackbrett*.

- The dudelzak (in German, "tootle sack") was a sheepskin or goatskin bag that had a chanter (melody pipe) that one blew into; it was similar in size to the French bagpipe (*musetett*), which was a favorite in aristocratic circles.
- The Judenleier, or Jewish hurdy-gurdy, was by the sixteenth century a lowly instrument associated with blind beggars, making it an option for poorer Jewish musicians.
- The positive, a fixed organ also called positive in English, stood on the floor or a table; the keys were close together. There was also the *portative*, whose straps the musician slung over the shoulder: it was used in processions and chamber music and was popular through the nineteenth century. Like the accordion, it was blown with one hand and played with the other.
- The Judenharfe (Jew's harp or *guimbard*) was played quite extensively in the Middle Ages, usually accompanying singers. The public often called the itinerant Jewish Polish musicians of the eighteenth century who played it *kharpe-shpilers* (Yiddish for "shameful players") because they played such a lowly, unpleasant sounding instrument; it was a play on words, a *kharpe* (instead of *harfe*) meant shameful in Hebrew. It was rarely played in a klezmer ensemble.
- The zink (in German, *Tusk*) was a kind of cornet, a slender curved instrument made from a goat's horn, usually with six bored holes, wrapped in black leather, with a trumpet mouthpiece. It was not an easy instrument to master because

the player's lips had to do much more to focus the pitch and give equality to the notes than with other wind and brass instruments. But with experience the player could produce a beautiful sound without equivalent today, mixing the qualities of the trumpet with the sweetness and agility of the oboe. It was popular from 1500–1650, after which the finest *zinkennistern* (cornetists) were attracted to the rapidly developing techniques of the violin.

• Lastly, the hackbrett (German for "cutting board"), sometimes called *Holzhar-monika* in German (or *hakbreydl* in Yiddish), was similar to the hammer dulcimer or *tsimbl*, that klezmer musicians in Central and Eastern Europe in the eighteenth century used widely. Sixteenth-century Italian Jews called it *dulce melos* (Italian for "sweet melody"). The famous hackbrett musician was the Polish klezmer Mikhl Joseph Guzikov (1806–1837); he played a Belorussian folk instrument called the *stroyfidl* (Yiddish for "straw fiddle") similar to the hackbrett, which he modified by increasing its range to two and a half octaves so that it was closer to today's xylophone. This portable instrument consisted of a set of solid wooden bars tuned diatonically and laid horizontally across a bed of cylindrically wound straw, which created the sound cavity. It was played by striking the bars with small wooden sticks.

There is a great deal of confusion about when the term *klezmer* began to be used to denote the Jewish musician rather than the instrument being played. In the Maharil of Mainz's (Jacob ben Moses Mollin, 1360–1427) book of marriage laws he used the word *klezmer* to denote musical instruments and *lets* to denote the musician when he wrote that the rabbi led the wedding procession, then came the groom followed by the letsim carrying their klezmer (referring to the instrument) to the synagogue courtyard before they went back for the bride. The earliest written references to the letsim are found in the writings of Talmudist Rabbi Elijah ben Isaac Lattes of Carcassonne, France, in the thirteenth century.[15] In another written source it stated that the Polish and Lithuanian Jews who immigrated to Holland in 1542 still referred to those playing Jewish music as letsim.

But by the eighteenth century, klezmer could also mean musician. In the first Yiddish songbook, Rabbi Elkhanan Kirchen's *Simkhat HaNefesh* (The Happiness of the Soul: Furth, 1707), Kirchen refers to the Jewish musician as a klezmer and a few years later in Hesse, Rabbi Khaiyim Yair wrote a statute (1690) that limited the kind of entertainers one could have at a wedding, saying that the letsim were a necessary part of the wedding as well as the servers but the luxury of having klezmers was forbidden.

From these and other sources it seems that the term *lets* was used fairly exclusively to denote the Jewish musician in Central and Eastern Europe as late as the sixteenth century. By the seventeenth century there are written sources that used the term *klezmer* instead of *lets*. But it was not until the nineteenth century that the word *klezmer*, or *musikant*,[16] was used fairly exclusively to represent the Jewish folk musician while the word *lets* meant only the wedding jester.

The batkhn was the Jewish folk bard who concentrated on song and story. He consoled the people by reading passages from the Torah and Talmud and by singing moralizing songs. His often semi-improvised rhyming poems were called *batkhones*, in which he combined the waggery and witticism of the lets with the leadership of the marshalik and the sharp intellect of the Talmudic scholar. He often recited or sang his batkhones unaccompanied but sometimes was joined by a klezmer (usually violin or tsimbl) or accompanied himself.

The Jewish Enlightenment movement was founded by the German Jew Moses Mendelssohn (1729–1786), who believed that the Jews who had been living for almost a thousand years walled in their ghettos should free their education of its religious shackles and strive for full civil emancipation. Mendelssohn and his devotees decided that the vernacular of Jews living in German lands should be German rather than Yiddish. Consequently, his proponents besmirched Yiddish as a corrupt jargon. Eventually, as the Jews became less religious and more emancipated, the function and style of music that the klezmer performed at weddings, engagements, and other celebrations shrank in popularity. By the middle of the nineteenth century, the batkhn, lets, marshalik, and klezmer had nearly disappeared in Germany, Austria, Moravia, Bohemia, and Holland. However, the klezmer had become an indispensable part of all Jewish celebrations and continued to flourish in the Yiddish-speaking centers of Eastern Europe lasting through the eve of World War II.

The advent of another Jewish philosophy, *Khasidim*,[17] founded by Israel ben Eliezer, the Ba'al Shem Tov (c.1700–c.1760), had an opposite effect on the Jews of Eastern Europe. Born in Mezritsh, Poland, in the Carpathian Mountains, the Ba'al Shem Tov was a healer, herbalist, and informed preacher who was able to have conversations with learned rabbis, rich Jews, simple Jews, and gentiles. He never wrote anything down, but his teachings and folk tales were transcribed by his disciples, who helped to spread his philosophy. The Ba'al Shem Tov's philosophy was completely the opposite of that of the *misnagidic* leader, the Vilna Gaon (Elijah ben Shlomo Zalman Kramer 1720–1797). The ascetic Talmudic rabbis lived caustic and regimented lives. Rejecting asceticism, the Ba'al Shem Tov emphasized joyfulness. The most direct way one could communicate one's joy to God was through prayer. Thus prayer filled with song (sometimes instrumental music and dancing) became the most essential way of reaching *dveykes*[18] to God.

Some Khasidim borrowed folk melodies and songs from their non-Jewish neighbors and created *nigunim*[19] with and without new text. Two of the more famous non-Jewish tunes that became part of the *Khasidic* repertoire are the Lubavitch *nign* "Napoleon's March" (sung to the melody of the Marseillaise) and the "Kalever Nign" (a Hungarian folk song called "Szol A Kakas Mar," or "The Rooster Is Already Crowing"). However most composed their own nigunim. The Khasidim left an indelible mark in the klezmer world with their impassioned singing and playing (both sometimes improvisational) and dancing. According to ethnomusicologist Walter Zev Feldman, their songs and dances helped make up the core dance repertoire, which had three sources: 1) older Central European dance music, which by the nineteenth century had largely blended with 2) dances based on the Ashkenazic prayer modes and Khasidic melodies and 3) Greco-Turkish dance music.[20] *Khasidism* was a boon for the spread of klezmer music throughout Eastern Europe.

The first time I heard the "Kalever Nign" I was traveling in eastern Slovakia, near Velki Kapusany, with a group of Hungarian Rom. To my astonishment they sang the song with the Hungarian and Hebrew words (the song is macaronic). I asked them where they had learned the song, but all they remembered was that it was a "holy Jewish song from a healer." Another time, in Satoraljauhely, in eastern Hungary, I met some Rom who knew the melody and words as well; they told me they had learned it while playing at Jewish celebrations before World War II.

Besides incorporating and re-creating indigenous folk tunes, Khasidim also composed their own nigunim, some, such as the Belzer, Bobover, Buhusher, Bratslaver, Moditser, Vishnitser, Stefuneshter, and Stoliner rabbis, becoming well known in the process. Others were famous for their musicianship, and a few even had their own klezmer ensembles, which generally only played at celebrations for the *rebe*[21] and his followers.

I am partial to the Stoliner nigunim because I grew up going to the Stoliner synagogue in Detroit and heard the melodies there and at home. My father's parents were followers of the Stoliner rebe, and his grandmother (my great-grandmother) was a close friend of Rabbi Israel Perlov (1873–1921), the Stoliner rebe known as the Yenuka (Hebrew for "baby") because he became the rebe just after his *bar mitsve*.[22]

While keeping with the Stoliner tradition of fervent praying, the rebe was also a great lover of music and continued the musical tradition of Stolin by having daily music in his home's courtyard. He also employed noted composers to compose new nigunim. The two best-known composers were Rabbi Jacob from Telekhan (near Pinsk, Belarus) and Rabbi Yossele Talner. The Stoliner rebe had two daughters and four sons; three of the sons formed a klezmer ensemble to play music for the celebrations in the courtyard.

In 1982, I had the good fortune to meet Asher Wainshteyn (1890–1983), who came from Stolin, when he was living in Boro Park, Brooklyn. He was a violinist in a klezmer band that also included a bassist, a *tsimbalist*, trumpeter, and a Belorussian drummer. They performed through the Pinsk, Belarus, region from 1906–1919, for Jews and gentiles alike. Wainshteyn immigrated after the Holocaust. He gave me a copy of his "gig" book, which contained ninety-four tunes. The variety of the melodies demonstrated the extensiveness of his repertoire; many of the tunes were not indigenous to the region, and these demonstrated how often the band played for gentiles. In his collection were tunes we call "core" repertoire, "transitional" repertoire, "co-territorial" repertoire, and "cosmopolitan" repertoire. Music in the core repertoire consisted of fixed choreographed dances like *freylekhs* and *khusidls*, rhythmic walking tunes like a *dobranotsh* or *gezegn*, and rubato tunes like a *baveynen* and *zogekhts*. The rubato melodies were performed for display at a wedding or were liturgical laments played before a holiday to heighten the spiritual awareness of the congregants. Sometimes this was on a festival like Khanike; other times it was for a holiday like

Yom Kippur. Wainshteyn performed a particular zogekhts for Rabbi Yisrael Perlow on the eve of Yom Kippur. The Khasidim's love of singing table songs (in Yiddish, *tish nigunim*) and songs they danced to like *skotshnes* (often melodies borrowed from the local peasants but then varied) widen the klezmer's repertoire.

The transitional repertoire came from the musical symbiosis of the Jewish klezmers and Roma musicians who lived and traveled in the Wallachia/Bessarabia, which today is part of Ukraine, Romania, and Moldova. Jewish and Roma musicians introduced dance tunes such as *volekh*, hora, *onge*, *sirba*, *bulgarish*, and *zhok*. The nondance tune introduced by these musicians that most likely had its origins in the Ottoman Empire is the *doyne*, also known earlier as the *taksim*. Though these are exclusively instrumental tunes, here too, the Khasidim in these regions had an influence on the repertoire. They sang wordless melodies to these very same dance tunes but at a much slower sometimes even rubato tempo in a rapturous, deep, contemplative voice.

The co-territorial repertoire came from songs and dances that originated from the local indigenous peasants. In the Ukraine this was the *kozatshok*, in Poland the mazurka, and in the Carpathian-Ruthenia the *kolomeyke*. The klezmer musicians (as well as the Roma) helped spread these tunes throughout Czarist Russia, the eastern part of Austro-Hungary, Wallachia, and Bessarabia.

Finally the cosmopolitan repertoire consisted of dance tunes that originated from Central and Western Europe, America, and even by the 1920s South America. These were melodies played for gentiles and Jews, particularly cosmopolitan Jews in the urban centers. These tunes were the lancer, cakewalk, *padespan*, *padekater*, polka, quadrille, tango, waltz, and others. Some of these tunes were excerpts based upon eighteenth- and nineteenth-century classical repertoire like the capriccio, minuet, bagatelle, polonaise, and others. While conducting ethnographic research in Berehove, Ukraine (known to the Jews as Beregszasz), I met a Roma woman, Ilinka, who played the piano. She remembered when traveling Yiddish theater troupes came through Berehove in the 1930s, and the klezmer musicians played various genres of music including classical. One tune she loved and learned to play was Pyotr Ilyich Tchaikovsky's "Valse Sentimentale" (composed in 1882), which she said was a favorite among Jews and Roma to have played at their weddings often for the newlyweds. The following are the different dances and melodies in Wainshteyn's gig book:

- The *dobranotsh* (Russian for "good night")—also known as the *dobranots* (Polish), *a gute nakht* (Yiddish for "good night"), *zay gezunt* (Yiddish for "be well"), or *gezegn* (Yiddish for "farewell")—was a piece, generally in a 4/4 time, played at the end of a wedding when the guests departed for home, often just before sunset; afterward the musicians accompanied the newlyweds and their parents to their respective homes with a march or sometimes a freylekhs.
- The *fantazi* (Yiddish for "fantasy") was a nondance tune often played at the table where the newlyweds and the parents sat and dined; like the classical musical

composition known as the fantasia, it had no fixed form, the structure being determined by the musician's or composer's fancy.

- The *hopke* was a lively Russian circle dance where one dancer danced within a bigger circle of dancers; it was very popular among the non-Jews.
- The *khusidl* (Hebrew for "little *Khasid*") was both a solo and a communal slow dignified Khasidic dance in 2/4 time that could be performed either in a circle or a line; however in Galicia, Transylvania, and the Carpathian regions of Hungary, it was considered the same as a freylekhs.
- The *koyletch tants* (Yiddish for "dance of the challah bread") incorporated a special twisted egg bread that was eaten on certain holidays and celebrations; it was performed immediately after the wedding ceremony was finished and thus was also called the *khupe tants* (Yiddish for "wedding canopy dance"). Usually the grandmother or another matriarch of the family danced in front of the bride and groom while holding the *koyletch* for all to see as the musicians accompanied them through the town to the wedding feast, all the while singing these words to the groom: "Vos vilstu: Di khale oder di kale?" (Yiddish for "What do you want: the bread or the bride?")
- The *mazltov tants* (Hebrew for "congratulations or good-luck dance"), also known as the *mitsve tants* (Hebrew for "good deed dance") and *kale tants* (Hebrew for "the bride dance"), was performed several times during the course of the wedding ceremony and feast. First it was performed when all the bride's female friends danced with her at the wedding canopy before the wedding ceremony; again after the groom veiled the bride, when the batkhn called out the women's names and each danced with the bride in turn in a stately circle while holding her hands and wishing her good luck; and again during the meal, when the batkhn called each of the honored guests by name to come up and congratulate the newlyweds, upon which the guests, in same-sex couples, danced to a melody in 3/4 or 3/8 time.
- The mazurka was an up-tempo Polish dance in 3/4 or 3/8 time, often with a "B" or trio section, and usually in a major key—native to the Mazovia region; it was quite popular in Western salons in the 1830s and '40s and was played as a sign of solidarity for partitioned Poland. It resembled the polka but had two sliding steps in place of one.
- The polka was an up-tempo dance in 2/4 time and a major key that originated in Bohemia around 1830. The basic step was a hop followed by three small steps; it could have two or three sections, with the last part a trio.
- The *padespan* (*pas d'espagnol*, in Spanish, meaning "Spanish step") was a Russian waltz based upon Spanish themes.
- The *sher* (Yiddish for "scissors") was one of the most common Jewish dances. According to Jewish ethnomusicologist Moishe Beregovski, it probably came from the German melody "Der Sherer oder Schartanz," which dates from 1562. It was a contradance in which from four to eight couples formed two facing lines; the couples bowed their heads toward each other as they switched places,

going under the gate formed by each other's arms. The Khasidim called the dance *hakhna'a* (Hebrew for "submission") because bowing one's head was a gesture of respect. The music was often a freylekhs in 2/4 time in a minor key, with two or three sections.

- The *skotshne* (Polish for "hop") was sometimes an instrumental display piece, but those Asher Wainshteyn played were like freylekhs in 2/4 time and in a minor key, except more technically elaborate; when dancing to them, the Khasidim incorporated hopping into their steps.
- The freylekhs (from the Yiddish word *frey*, "happy") was the most common upbeat klezmer dance in 2/4 or sometimes 4/4 time. It always had three sections and was generally played in a minor key.
- The *tish-nign* (Yiddish for "table song") was a Khasidic wordless melody sung with great spirituality, sometimes at the rebe's table, when the rebe and his followers welcomed the Sabbath with songs on Friday night, and other times sung by the batkhn while the wedding guests were dining. The accompaniment was a solo instrument, usually violin, which played rubato.
- The waltzes that were in Wainshteyn's manuscript were arranged from popular classical melodies of the day as well as from Russian and Polish folk songs. One of the most popular waltzes Wainshteyn's ensemble was asked to play at both Jewish and non-Jewish celebrations was Tchaikovsky's "Waltz Sentimentale" (opus 52, number 6).
- The zogekhts (Yiddish for "to say") was a display piece in which the klezmer utilized a synagogue prayer motif to compose an improvisational piece in rubato rhythm. Occasionally it segues into a khusidl, like the zogekhts in the Wainshteyn manuscript that was sung to the prayer "V'hee Sheyomda Lavotseynu" (Hebrew for "And He Stood for Us"), which was often sung during the holiday of Passover. When the zogekhts was sung, the singer often used coloratura (trills, runs, scales), a vocal technique that the cantor also used.
- The cakewalk, an African American folk dance from the late nineteenth and early twentieth centuries, was a strutting dance step originally developed for competing for a cake. The two cakewalks in the Wainshteyn manuscript had three sections, the first two in minor and the third, a trio in a major key.[23]

Much of the traditional klezmer music performed today is based on the music of the Jewish musicians who came from Belarus, Lithuania, Poland, Ukraine, and Russia, and this style of klezmer playing and repertoire is called the Polish-Ukrainian. The other dominant style (and some would say the most prevalent and influential today) is called Romanian-Turkish, with klezmer music and style of playing by musicians who came from what is Eastern Hungary today, the Carpathian region and Romania including the former Romanian provinces of Bukovina and Bessarabia.

While the klezmer musicians in the Czarist army performed marches, waltzes, and pieces in other musical genres, the repertoire in Romania, the eastern parts of the Austro-Hungarian Empire and Ottoman Empire represented more of a near Eastern sound. In Constantinople, many members of the significant Ashkenazic minority living among the much larger Sephardic community were ancestors of those who came from Ukraine and Poland seeking refuge during the Chmielnicki pogroms (1648–1649) and Great Deluge. Others came at the end of the eighteenth century searching for better economic opportunities, while still others had been traveling to Palestine, stopped on the way, and stayed.

After Europe was able to defeat the Ottoman Turks in 1699, the Ottomans ceded most of Hungry, Slavonia, and Transylvania to the Habsburg Empire and Podolia to Poland. Some klezmer musicians from southern Poland and the lands of Bohemia and Moravia found new economic opportunities in Hungary playing alone and with the local Roma. In 1867 when the Austro-Hungarian Empire emancipated the Jews, many musicians in the more developed western part of the empire sought better paying jobs, while others assimilated along with many of their fellow brethren in Budapest, Prague, Brno, etc. However in Ottoman Moldavia and Czarist Bessarabia the Jews on the whole were not assimilating. Jewish daily life was still under the influence of the local rabbis or rebes. There the Jewish and Roma musicians often playing in each other's ensembles found plenty of work.

Constantinople was the nexus of several major trade routes—going north to Odessa via the Black Sea; west to Vienna via the Danube River through Galati, Belgrade, and Budapest; and south to Jerusalem. For the Jewish musicians living in Constantinople between the mid-nineteenth century and the beginning of World War I, these trade routes gave them easy access to a variety of places, and traveling these routes enabled them to pick up new tunes (particularly from Roma musicians traveling the same routes) and teach their own to others.

One of the major sources that created the klezmer's core dance repertoire was Greco-Turkish dance music. The Middle Eastern modes were already familiar to the klezmer (from synagogue prayer), as were the improvisational, melismatic singing and playing exhibited in many of the tunes. But by the beginning of the nineteenth century the repertoire of the Roma musicians was involved. The repository for this mixing, exchanging, and borrowing of Greco-Turkish tunes was the region of Moldavia/Bessarabia. Dance tunes such as the *hong, sirba,* zhok, and *bulgarish* and display tunes such as the *Terkishe* freylekhs, *Terkishe gebet, vulekhl, doyne,* and taksim now formed the core of the Romanian-Turkish klezmer sound. This Greco-Turkish influence became very apparent to me when I was in Chisinau, Moldova (Kishinev), and my Roma friend Nikolai Radu began to play a melody on the piano he learned from Jewish musicians while playing at weddings before World War II in Bessarabia. He called the melody a *ketsev tants* (Yiddish for "butcher's dance," from the Hebrew word for butcher) that melodically and rhythmically sounded like the Greek folk dance called *Hasapiko.* It originated in Constantinople during the Middle Ages when Greek butchers danced with swords sometimes before going into battle.

The capital for the Polish-Ukrainian sound was Berditshev (Berdiciv, Ukraine), where, near the end of the nineteenth century, there were over fifty klezmer musicians, among them several klezmer virtuosi who led bands that became legendary throughout the southwest part of Ukraine and eastern Galicia. The capital of the Romanian-Turkish sound was Iasi, Romania, which from the mid-nineteenth century through the eve of World War II was the home of several virtuosi and their bands famous throughout Moldavia and Bessarabia.

To learn more about the history of klezmer in Iasi and its environs, I traveled there many times, met with many retired klezmer musicians, including several Roma who played in klezmer bands, and spoke to the world's leading authority on Moldavian/ Bessarabian Jewish culture, Itsik "Kara" Svarţ (1906–2001). His account exhibits the richness of Jewish culture in Moldavia and Bessarabia before World War II, and how vital it was to the development of Romanian klezmer:

> I was born in Podu Iloaiei, just outside of Iasi. In my town there were no Jewish klezmers but in Iasi there were many ensembles. So when there was a wedding we brought them from Iasi by train. When we did not, we hired the Gypsies. These Gypsy klezmers knew Jewish music very well and played at all our local balls and for the Jewish festivals. On Purim they went from house to house accompanying the Purimshpilers [Yiddish for "Purim actors"]. The Jews were not ignorant klezmers[;] they all knew how to read notes. And by the 1920s most klezmer in this region read music because they had gone to the conservatory.
>
> Several ensembles, particularly the famous Sigally and Bughici families, made a good living only from music. This was rare for most of the klezmers, but in Iasi with the Yiddish theatre, outdoor garden cafes, restaurants, weddings, parties, and the movie theatre in the 1930s, there were many opportunities for the klezmers to find work. The Yiddish theatre where I worked as a translator and dramaturge had an orchestra made up only of klezmers.
>
> The reputation of most klezmers prior to 1920 was not a good one. The klezmer was looked upon like an actor or circus entertainer who lived a Bohemian life, so the public expressed a great deal of uneasiness about him.
>
> In the 1800s the Jewish klezmers of Moldavia played in the court of Prince Linye. He said: "The Jews of Moldavia are the best musicians, businessmen, and brokers." In the mid-1800s some klezmers from Galicia traveled throughout Moldavia introducing the local Jews and non-Jews to Jewish and non-Jewish music from Poland and from south-western Ukraine. But the greatest influence, one that can still be heard today from the few who play klezmer, was that of Balkan music. Throughout the 1800s Jewish, Roma, Greek and Romanian musicians traveled often to Constantinople. There they played Jewish and all kinds of other music and brought back new Turkish tunes which they introduced to the public. The klezmers played the Turkish music the best because they already knew the scales from many of their synagogue prayers.
>
> Before World War II in Iasi we had several well-known klezmer ensembles that either originally came from Iasi or from the Moldavia-Bessarabia region. They were the Lemesi, Bughici, and Sigally family bands. The Lemesi ensemble originally came from Balti (Moldova today). They played Romanian klezmer music during the reign of Czar Alexander II, who was very harsh against the Jews and Romanians. The Lemesi ensemble had a wide reputation, and when the Italian Opera Company came to Bucharest to play in the Romanian National Theatre they asked that the Lemesi ensemble be part of the pit orchestra.

The violinists in the Lemesi, Sigally and Bughici klezmer bands were great talents, but the most famous of all klezmer violinists in Romania was Jacob Psanter (1828–1896). He was the oldest child in his family and had to support them after his father died when he was very young. He played by ear and performed for the Jews, and non-Jews, poor and rich. Though he knew his work was considered a low profession he never regretted having become a klezmer. He wrote in a book published in 1875 that had he been a religious Jew he would have been very learned in Torah and as famous for his rabbinical skills as he was for his violin.

After World War I most klezmers in Iasi were not religious but you could still find some with long beards and *payes* [Yiddish for "earlocks"] in a few towns and villages like Buhusi. The Buhusher rebe had his own klezmer band that played at all the religious affairs in the town. The rebe's Buhusher nign is quite known throughout Moldavia among the Jews. I even grew up singing it on Friday nights.[24] Finally the introduction of the gramophone in the late '20s hurt the small bands. Instead of hiring a band for a dance or to play in a restaurant or café, people played the gramophone. Of course the rich always could afford the best and they kept the Sigally and Bughici bands busy until the war began.[25]

The mainstay for the klezmer was the Jewish wedding. But despite the klezmer's importance at a Jewish wedding, his social standing in the Jewish community was rather fluid, and sometimes his social standing was just a rung or two higher than the local porters. Playing music generally paid poorly, thus making it difficult for the klezmer to provide for his family. *Klezmorim* were looked upon as not being close followers of or learned in the Torah and Talmud. And to compound things, even though klezmorim traveled less at the turn of the twentieth century than they had in the early nineteenth, the impression of their being usually away from home stuck, leading to suspicions and rumors that they fraternized with all types of unsavory Jewish and gentile people like drunks, thieves, prostitutes, smugglers, and gamblers. Finally to make the Jewish community even more apprehensive and wary, the klezmorim even had their own argot—klezmer *loshn* (Yiddish for "klezmer language"), which they used both at Jewish and non-Jewish festivities. The klezmorim used this argot specifically so they could speak in secret in front of the people they met while traveling and the people they played for. The conversations were often filled with sarcasm, disdain, humor, and sexual innuendo.

The majority of the klezmer musicians at the end of the nineteenth century lived in the Pale of Settlement, a territory in Czarist Russia established in 1905, which comprised 20 percent of the total area of European Russia. Most Polish and Russian Jews (with the rare exception of some high school graduates, wealthy merchants, doctors, and ex-cantonists) were forced to live within this crowded (5,500,000 Jews in 1900), economically depressed area of twenty-five provinces from 1835 to 1915. Unfortunately, because of the power and popularity of such films as *Fiddler on the Roof* and *Yentl*, the image of Jewish life in the towns and villages in the Pale has been distorted beyond recognition. Yes, there were some idyllic, nostalgic times, but they were mixed with a good measure of daily rigors. Poverty was a constant companion, the streets and alleys were often muddy and fetid, the outlying areas were often swampy, winters

were harsh with snow and freezing temperatures, summers were replete with swelter-
ing heat and swarms of mosquitoes, rabbis passed religious laws that other rabbis
overruled, and coexistence with the non-Jewish neighbors was an up-and-down affair,
depending on the level of local anti-Semitism.

Because of the klezmer's fluctuating social position in the Jewish community and
the often bleak economic situation, many klezmer bands took care of each other in
times of need, even if they did not have a union or a guild to support them.[26] If a
klezmer was sick and not able to perform at a job, he was still paid a full portion.
"His life was our life. His problem, our problem. His fate, our fate."[27] The klezmer
who stopped working because he was too old or had an injury and was not able to
find another job was still paid a percentage of his former band's share. If the klezmer
died and his widow was old and did not have any children, then she received her
husband's full salary if the band could afford it. If they could not, then she received
a percentage of his former salary. If the widow had children and they were too young
for work, then she received half her husband's salary, or some other percentage. The
following account exemplifies this klezmer kinship:

> I had left Rahov [Rahiv, Ukraine] early in the morning on my way to visit my brother
> who lived in Kassau [Kosice, Slovakia]. The train stopped in Munkacs [Mukaceve,
> Ukraine] because it was having some engine problems. It wasn't going to be until the next
> morning that the engine would be repaired. It was summertime—very hot and humid.
> I didn't want to stay in my seat inside the train the whole night. It was like a furnace.
> I went inside where I saw three klezmer musicians playing. I knew they were klezmers
> because I heard them speaking Yiddish mixed with a little klezmer slang. There was an
> accordionist, violinist, and saxophonist. The violinist came up to me having seen my
> violin on the floor next to me. I told him what had happened and why I was in Munkacs
> for the night. Immediately he invited me to stay that night in his home. He had an extra
> bed and he lived only a few blocks away from the station. He and his wife were very nice
> and I slept very well. I meant to keep in contact with him but I never did. After the war,
> I was visiting Munkacs on business and asked about the violinist. He died in Auschwitz
> (Oswiecim), Poland.[28]

In the Czarist army Jews were not only introduced to wind instruments, but many
also learned how to read and arrange music. There was not much room in a czarist
military band for string players, so many klezmer violinists became trumpeters to
avoid combat. After being discharged from the army some of these Jewish musicians
were able to parlay their new musical talents to higher social standing and better-
paying jobs, such as playing in the fireman's brigade band and/or semi-professional
orchestras, or teaching children whose parents (Jewish and non-Jewish) could afford
private lessons. Their years of playing in the military bands also changed the makeup
of the klezmer ensembles in Europe starting in the mid-nineteenth century, whose
woodwind-and-brass sounds (sometimes led by a violinist) crossed over the Atlantic
by the end of the nineteenth century. Hence the woodwind and brass instrumentation influenced the repertoire and makeup of the klezmer ensembles in America.
These ensembles could be as large as fifteen musicians, and be a combination of

violin, bass, clarinet, flute, piccolo, cornet, trumpet, trombone, alto saxophone, tuba (or alto or baritone), snare, cymbals, and a woodblock.

The most famous klezmer musician to have served in the Czar's army was clarinetist Dave Tarras, who was drafted in 1915 as Europe was engulfed in World War I. Tarras recalls:

> I was seventeen when I enlisted in the army. The commander liked my music very much and he put me in the band. He was a German but still fought for the Czar. He called me and said "Tarras, what else do you play?" I told him I play a little mandolin. The next day while eating lunch he called the whole mandolin orchestra. He gave me a mandolin and he asked me to play a solo. After I played the solo I got a big applause. In about two days he sent me to Petersburg to buy some instruments. He sent one of the soldiers from the band with me to buy a new clarinet, violin, a guitar and a mandolin. At that time the soldiers were getting ninety cents a month. And immediately the German officer gave an order that Tarras should be paid ten dollars a month. This was unbelievable. Being in the regiment under the music commander was like the golden ring for me. They all gave me a lot of respect and they worked for me. Sometimes at night the officers used to drink. One of these officers was a good singer so they would send a soldier with two horses for me. They wanted me to accompany the officer who sang on the guitar. And of course I never saw any shooting, nothing. I had a revolver but it didn't mean anything.[29]

One hundred years later, the opportunity to fulfill one's military obligation by playing in the military band rather than serving in a combat unit remains viable. As one klezmer told me: "When I was nine I could already play the piano and read music, but my mother wanted me to be a woodwind player so that when I had to serve my mandatory military service in the Red Army, I would be in the military band instead of being sent to fight in the Afghanistan war."[30]

After Nicholas I's death, Alexander II (1856–1881) decided to follow a more liberal policy concerning the Jews and issued amnesties and suspensions of taxes and fines. He also ended the conscription of Jewish children and liberalized educational policies for Jews. Those who had obtained a higher education were allowed to live outside the Pale. Consequently the number of Jews enrolled in the universities increased, including some klezmer musicians who could not formally study music at the new and prestigious music conservatories in St. Petersburg and Odessa. These and other liberal reforms helped the enlightenment to penetrate even the most remote and religiously controlled Jewish communities in the Pale's hinterlands, they also encouraged many Jews to adopt Russian culture and practice less of their own.

By the end of the nineteenth century the severe economic situation in the Pale forced more and more klezmer musicians to work as artisans or day laborers. They could only play klezmer music part-time. If a band traveled it was usually no more than a half-day's ride by horse and wagon. This is not to say there were not klezmer musicians that could not solely provide for their families only by playing music, but this was the exception rather than the rule.

In 1881, the political atmosphere became more oppressive, especially for the Jews, when Czar Alexander II was assassinated, and the Russian authorities blamed it on the

Jews. Subsequently the Czarist government tried to divert attention from the political and economic woes the country was experiencing (that were especially harsh for the peasants) by blaming the Jews for these societal disasters as well. Decades of pogroms ensued against the Jewish population and made life unpredictable and unbearable. Consequently anti-Semitism and deplorable economic conditions drove millions of Jews from Eastern Europe. They came from the Pale of Settlement (modern Poland, Lithuania, Belarus, Ukraine, and Moldova) and the Russian-controlled portions of Poland. Approximately two million Yiddish-speaking Jews immigrated to the United States. Among them were several thousand klezmer musicians who would soon be plying their trade in the United States, specifically in New York City and its environs.

NOTES

1. I Samuel 16:23.

2. Abraham Z. Idelsohn, *Jewish Music: Its Historical Development* (New York: Henry Holt, 1929), 93.

3. The word comes from two Hebrew words, *kley* and *zmer*. *Kley* means vessels or tools, and *zmer* means melody. In Yiddish, the word *klezmer* literally means vessels of the music. *Klezmer* in Central and Eastern Europe before the seventeenth century meant a musical instrument. By the mid-seventeenth century the word had begun to be used to denote the Jewish musician. And by the eighteenth century throughout Central and Eastern Europe, *klezmer* meant the Jewish folk instrumentalist. His music was a specific kind of Ashkenazic folk music, which was primarily dance music. Today the definition has broadened and means Ashkenazic dance, vocal, and melismatic instrumental music.

4. *Minnesinger* (Ger.): itinerant German lyric poet and singer of the twelfth to the fourteenth centuries.

5. *Spielleuter* (Ger.): playing person, an itinerant German musician.

6. *Jongleur* (Fr.): itinerant French musician from the eleventh to thirteenth centuries. They traveled throughout France and Norman England singing lyric songs and reciting epic stories accompanying themselves often with the lute or cittern.

7. *Shpilman* (Yid.): gleeman.

8. Joachim Stutschevsky, *Ha-Klezmorim Toldotehem OrakhHayehem v'Yezirotchem* (Jerusalem: Bialik Institute, 1959), 35.

9. Paul Nettl, *Alte jüdische Shpielleute und Musiker* (Prague: Dr. J. Flesch, 1923), 41.

10. *Lets* (*letsim* pl.; Heb.): clown, jester, buffoon.

11. *Possenreiser* (Ger.): jester, buffoon.

12. *Nar* (*narim* pl.; Yid.): fool, clown.

13. *Marshalik* (Yid.): marshal, wedding jester, master of ceremonies.

14. *Batkhn* (Yid.): wedding bard, originally from the Aramaic *bada*, which means to make merry. His often semi-improvisational rhyming poems were called *batkhones* or *shtey-gramen* (Yiddish stand-up rhymes) where he combined the waggery and witticism of the lets with the leaderhip of the marshalik and the sharp intellect of the Talmudic scholar (student of Jewish oral law consisting of the interpretation of the laws contained in the Torah). Like the klezmer, many *batkhonim* inherited the job from their father, grandfather, or uncle.

15. "Merrymakers at a Jewish Wedding," *YIVO Annual Jewish Social Science*, ed. Ezekiel Lifschutz, VII (1952): 44.

16. *Musikant* (Yid.): musician. By the nineteenth century in Eastern Europe the Jewish musician was either referred to as a musikant or as a klezmer.

17. *Khasidim* (Heb.): pious ones. Those Jews who are followers of the *khasidic* movement.

18. *Dveykus* (Heb.): adhesion.

19. *Nign* (*nigunim* pl.; Yid.): melody. Generally a wordless melody often sung by the khasidim.

20. "Khevrisa: European Klezmer Music," *Smithsonian Folkways Recording* (liner notes), Walter Zev Feldman (2000), 5.

21. *Rebe* (*Rabeiim* pl.; Heb.): a spiritual leader of a particular khasidic sect.

22. *Bar mitsve* (Heb.): the religious ceremony whereby a thirteen-year-old Jewish boy becomes a young adult in the Jewish community.

23. Wainshteyn explained to me that a man from Pinsk, a friend of the *tsimbler*'s, had visited America around 1910 and brought back some sheet music, including these two cakewalks.

24. The earliest known written record of this tune I found in this book. Emil Saculet, *Yidishe Folks-Lider* (Bucharest: Editura Muzicala, 1959).

25. Interview with Itsik "Kara" Svarṭ (originally from Podu Iloaiei, Romania) in Iasi, Romania, Februrary 23, 1985. (Itsik wrote under the pen name "Kara," which means black in Turkish, because his last name Svart, means black in Yiddish.)

26. Klezmer musicians formed guilds to help each other and to have more strength as a unified group, especially when they had to fight the various edicts and restrictions that the non-Jewish authorities constantly placed upon them. The earliest klezmer guild we know of was started in Prague in 1558 and another in Lublin in 1654.

27. Interview with Dumitru Bughici (originally from Iasi, Romania) in Bucharest, Romania, March 13, 1985.

28. Interview with Shaiya Shindelman (originally from Rahiv, Ukraine) in Hust, Ukraine, August 17, 1997.

29. Yale Strom, *Dave Tarras: The King of Klezmer* (Kfar Sava, Israel: Or-Tav Music Publications, 2010), 15.

30. Interview with Leo Chelyapov (originally from Moscow), in Los Angeles, California, June 12, 2000.

2

A History of Klezmer from the Twentieth Century to the Present

Yale Strom

Between 1880 and 1924, nearly one-third of East European Jewry, most from Czarist Russia and Poland, emigrated from their homelands, the majority to America, in the largest movement of Jews since the Spanish Inquisition. Wretched poverty, pervasive anti-Semitism, and violent pogroms gave the Jews ample reason to seek a better life in the United States.

Jewish life in Eastern Europe might have been confining to many Jews, but life in America, particularly in the urban centers, was chaotic. Until 1914, when the United States government halted legal immigration, a renewable source of Yiddish-speaking Jews continued to immigrate to America. But after the doors to Ellis Island were closed and assimilation for many Jews became a means to an end, Yiddish culture in America began to recede rapidly, evolving from a necessity of Jewish life to a nostalgic memory for the immigrant and finally to a piece of clothing that no longer fit.

In this chaotic urban cauldron, the immigrant tried to make a living. Though most klezmers had struggled with poverty and their fluctuating social status in Eastern Europe, they nevertheless had a specific and important role to perform in the Jewish community. In America, though, immigrants were immediately thrust into a bewildering industrial society, one that either gave them opportunity to succeed economically if they had the willpower, physical strength, and luck, or one that swallowed them whole with all its vices of graft, gambling, prostitution, and alcoholism.

The intense concentration of Jews in New York City meant overcrowded and filthy tenement houses, unemployed sweatshop workers, peddlers, and beggars. The streets and courtyards provided plenty of easy-access venues and earning possibilities for the new immigrant klezmer who did not yet have a job. Just as he had in urban centers like Warsaw, Lemberg (L'viv), Kiev, Minsk, and Berditshev, the klezmer played in the tenement courtyards as the neighborhood itinerant minstrel. As one witness told me:

I remember when I was eight we lived on Ludlow St. This klezmer fiddler would come around to our yard around seven a.m., just after most of the men had gone to work. He didn't carry a case for the violin. He carried [it] just under his arm with the bow. As he played a slow waltz, suddenly the wives would lean out of their apartment windows with a smile, enjoying the music. Then, after maybe two or three minutes, these women went back inside their homes and returned with some money. After the tune was finished, they clapped and threw some coins down. It was usually a few pennies, a nickel, or, if he was really lucky, a dime. But what I remember most was that some of the women also threw down small pieces of rolled-up paper. The klezmer gathered these as well, stuffed them into his pocket, and left. When I told a friend of mine what I had seen he said it was probably the women giving him the different times of the day when their husbands came home from work. But later I found out that on these pieces of paper were numbers which corresponded with certain racehorses. He was running these numbers over to a bookie who then placed small bets for the women.[1]

For most klezmers in Eastern Europe, the Jewish wedding had been the "bread and butter" gig, with celebrations generally held in a home or synagogue courtyard and lasting seven days. Weddings were equally important for the immigrant klezmer, but were smaller, usually just one day (except for the Orthodox Jews who observed the tradition of the "seven blessings over seven days"), and held in social and catering halls. Some catering halls had house bands; those klezmers lucky enough to be employed by one had a certain amount of economic security. However this made it difficult for the "greenhorn" klezmer who had just come off the ship to find employment. There was still a sense of brotherhood among the klezmers in America, but because of economic pressures and lack of work musicians held on to their catering and social club jobs tightly and did not welcome competitors.

> Catering halls formed the site for a range of large-scale entertainment and public events including weddings, *bar mitsves*, charity balls, social dances, and political meetings. They held hundreds of people at full capacity, and the Lower East Side teemed with them. Klezmers found themselves in catering halls for a variety of events, and performed for different immigrant ethnic groups. But it was the Jewish wedding which continued to define much of the character of their work, and the Jewish wedding in America was profoundly determined by the catering hall.[2]

Just as, back in Eastern Europe, the klezmer had to be versed in several folk genres (Bessarabian, Hungarian, Lithuanian, Polish, Roma, Romanian, Russian, Ruthenian, Slovakian, and Ukrainian), in America he had to be equally well versed, or even better. On the Lower East Side many different ethnic groups lived and worked side by side. And though the core audience for the klezmers were Jews, they had to know other genres of music, as non-Jews often hired them for weddings and parties.

In 1916 Wolff N. Kostakowsky published his klezmer anthology *Hebrew International Wedding Music*, which contained three hundred tunes (Hungarian, Jewish, Polish, Romanian, Russian) that formed the core repertoire of tunes these immigrants knew from the old country. Then in 1924, twins Joseph and Jack Kammen published the first of several music books that became the "fake books" for all klezmer musicians. On the cover of these books it stated that they contained American, Bessarabian, Bulgarian, Greek, Gypsy, Hungarian, Italian, Jewish, Polish, Romanian, Russian, Serbian, and Ukrainian tunes. Some of the tunes were actual folk melodies and songs from these countries and regions, but many of them were Yiddish folk songs and klezmer tunes that were performed with nuances as they were, for example, of Greek or Serbian origin.

Dance halls, which had created the need for klezmer music back in the twelfth through fourteenth centuries, again provided work opportunities at the turn of the twentieth century. They were popular among early immigrants because they provided a place to socialize with the opposite sex, to learn English, and to acculturate more easily into American society. Some dance halls played predominately music from Europe, the mazurka, lancer, polka, quadrille, *sher*, and tarantella. But most of the dance halls and dance schools (as portrayed in the film *Hester Street*, for example) played and taught ragtime, society dances, and in the 1920s and '30s, big band swing and tango. Some klezmers were not able to play American popular music as well as their old repertoire. For some it was because they could not read music, and the genre was foreign to their ears. Others felt that since there were plenty of other musicians who had played this new music longer and better, why would someone hire a klezmer who only played it so-so?

Another tradition that immigrants brought with them to America was that of getting out of the hectic, crowded, and all-too-often foul-aired city for the fresh air and serenity of the country. In Bohemia, Jews (even those of modest means) who lived in Galicia and Carpathian-Ruthenia had frequented the resorts of Marienbad and Karslbad, rejuvenating themselves with the fresh air and mineral baths.

As early as 1890, a few East European and German Jews began going up to the Catskill Mountains to escape the humid confines of summers in New York City. (There were existing resorts in the area, but they generally prohibited Jews, so the Jews built their own.) By 1902 the Yiddish press began advertising Catskill resorts catering specifically to the East European Jewish immigrant. In the beginning, most were just plain boardinghouses grouped together around a lake and a small patch of forest. Eventually most of these gave way to fancier hotels. The hotels dotting the Catskills landscape hired klezmer musicians to play, mostly for dances and background music during dinner. The ensembles often consisted, in various combinations, of violin, piano, accordion, clarinet, trumpet, saxophone, and drums. The repertoire included klezmer, light European classical, American popular dance music, and beginning in the 1920s, a strain of music that mixed American popular song arrangements with nostalgic Yiddish lyrics and some klezmer nuances.

By the 1930s the entertainment at the various Catskill resorts included comedy, comedic skits, Yiddish/English one-act plays, and music revues. The *batkhonim* of Eastern Europe had ceased to exist for the most part in the United States (except among the *Khasidim*) and were now replaced by "Borscht Belt *toomlers*."[3] Combining jokes, music, song, and dance, such performers as Joey Adams, Milton Berle, Georgie Jessel, Jan Murray, and later Fyvush Finkel, Buddy Hackett, Danny Kaye, and Jerry Lewis became modern-day batkhonim.

Besides comedians, other entertainers—musicians and singers—also got their start performing in the Catskills. As klezmer clarinetist Marty Levitt recalled: "My father Jack was a trombonist who played at the Presidents Hotel when it first opened in Swan Lake, New York in 1932. The leader of the band was Jan Peerce, who played the violin. On certain tunes Peerce would put down the violin and sing; but the people in the audience yelled at him to play the violin instead. Of course he made it as an opera singer, not as a violinist."[4]

Some of these same klezmer musicians, when not playing in the Catskills during summer, were part of a developing recording industry. Some of the early labels were Syrena, Pathe, Emerson, Columbia, and Gramophone Company. Klezmer music in Eastern Europe had been recorded since the late 1890s, so it only made sense that the burgeoning Jewish immigrant population in America would want to listen to recordings that filled them with nostalgia for their former homelands.

Abe Elenkrig (1878–1965), with his klezmer ensemble the Hebrew Bulgarian Orchestra, was one of the earliest to record klezmer tunes. The band's sound was a brassy, very rhythmic sound with a strong connection to the Romanian folk music of Moldavia and the brass-band sound of southwestern Ukraine. There was Harry Kandel (1885–1943), who studied clarinet at the conservatory in Odessa. His ensemble simulated the military marching-band sound. After a short stint in New York City, Kandel moved to Philadelphia, first playing under John Philip Sousa and then becoming the pit conductor for the Yiddish plays and vaudeville shows at the Arch Street Theatre. From 1917 to 1927 Kandel recorded a slew of records, many of which became the standards of their day. Like the klezmer musicians back in Eastern Europe that adapted their repertoires in response to the times and locations (the Romanian shepherd's *doyne* became a standard part of the Jewish wedding repertoire), Kandel's large-wind-ensemble recordings attempted to fuse klezmer with jazz elements. These became seminal recordings for the revival klezmer bands in the 1970s and early '80s; some of his more noted klezmer recordings include "Di Mama Iz Gegangen in Mark Arayn" (Yiddish for "The Mother Has Gone to the Market"), "Der Shtiler Bulgar" (Yiddish for "The Quiet Bulgar"), and "Mamliga." For his foray into jazz, Kandel changed the instrumentation of his band, adding three saxophones and a tenor banjo. His most famous *jazzmer* tune was "Jakie, Jazz 'em Up," recorded in 1926 under the heading Kandel's Jazz Orchestra. Typically these tunes were played as a swing tune with a klezmer trumpet break in the middle and/or at the end of the piece.

The Jakie in the aforementioned title was Jacob "Jakie" Hoffman (1899–1974), who played percussion in Kandel's band and also helped to create the Philadelphia klezmer sound. Hoffman transposed the sound and method of playing the *tsimbl* to the louder xylophone and can be heard on several recordings, including: "Firn Di Mekhutonim Aheym" (Yiddish for "Leading the In-Laws Home") and "Der Gas Nign" (Yiddish for "The Street Tune"). A xylophone virtuoso, Hoffman played with several symphony orchestras, including the Philadelphia Orchestra and Boston Pops. His daughter, Elaine Hoffman Watts, followed in her father's footsteps and became a percussionist playing classical (Philadelphia Orchestra) and klezmer. Her daughter

Susan has continued the family klezmer tradition and is a well-known trumpet player and Yiddish vocalist.

Other klezmer ensemble leaders during the golden age of Yiddish popular music who made recordings include Joseph Rimshinsky (1879–1956), I. J. Hochman, Lt. Joseph Frankel (1885–1953; he served in both the Czarist and United States armies), Joseph Cherniavsky (1895–1959), and Abe Schwartz (1881–1963). Joseph Cherniavsky's Yiddishe American Jazz Band (also known as the Hassidic American Jazz Band) dressed as Cossacks and Khasidim and played jazz versions of klezmer tunes. However Schwartz may have been the most successful of these leaders. Born in a small town outside of Bucharest, he came to the United States in 1899 and soon thereafter became a leader in the klezmer scene. A violinist, pianist, arranger, composer, and bandleader, he performed on several of his own recordings, including a few on which he played solo violin accompanied only by his daughter Sylvia on piano. Some of the famous tunes he composed and/or arranged were "Orientalische Hora" (Yiddish for "Oriental Hora," 1919), "Shwer un Shweeger Tantz" (Yiddish for "In-Law's Dance," 1921), "Di Grine Kuzine" (Yiddish for "The Greenhorn Cousin," 1922), and "Romanian Volach" ("Descend," 1922). And by the late 1920s on many of the klezmer recordings one could hear the virtuoso clarinet playing of Naftuli Brandwine and David Tarras, both of whom set the standard for klezmer clarinet playing.

With the Jewish immigrant masses (some two million Yiddish speakers) wanting more klezmer and jazzmer music, one did not have to own a phonograph but only had to turn on the radio to listen to one of several Yiddish radio programs. Yiddish radio flourished nationwide. In New York alone, twenty-three stations broadcast a variety of programs including recorded and live music. Such stations as WHN, WBBC, WBNX, and the leader WEVD (subsidized and eventually owned by the *Forverts* newspaper), were great venues from the 1920s to its decline in the mid '50s for the most popular Yiddish singers and klezmer musicians: Dave Tarras, Abe Ellstein, Aaron Lebedeff, Molly Picon, Max Epstein, Sammy Muziker, and others. The exposure broadened their reputations, sold their records, and secured more work for them.

Probably the most successful of the klezmer musicians who performed both in the klezmer and jazz worlds was Sammy Musiker (1916–1963). Descended from a family of klezmers, Musiker played both tenor saxophone and clarinet in Gene Krupa's band in the late 1930s and early '40s. In 1941 Sammy married Brouny Tarras, Dave's oldest daughter. Immediately Dave Tarras welcomed his new son-in-law to the family and his klezmer world. On September 21–22, 1955, Epic Records (then part of Columbia Records) brought Tarras together with Sammy and Ray Musiker (Sammy's brother) as well as Melvin Solomon on trumpet, Carl Prager and Phil Bodner on reeds, Seymour Megenheimer on accordion, Moe Wechsler on piano, Mack Shopnick on contrabass, and Irving Graetz on percussion to create an album that bridged the early immigrant years with the conservative 1950s. This album was called *Tanz!* Today many klezmer historians and *bale-kulturniks* (Yiddish for "masters of culture")[5] designate this album as one of the first and best of the revival klezmer albums to begin to merge klezmer with swing. It was an album of dance tunes that were essentially played for concert listening. Each side of the disc featured Tarras and Sam Musiker playing clarinet together on some tunes, individually on other tunes; some of which were traditional, while others were original tunes composed by Musiker specifically for the album. The album was far ahead of its time, and ultimately *Tanz!* was a concept album and did not sell well. It did not attract the Jewish audiences who wanted to hear only traditional klezmer, and it did not attract jazz listeners who wanted to hear Tarras's modal soli and improvisation as his playing is rather controlled on the album.

Though Jewish jazz really did not find its niche among the American public and record companies, a few Jewish tunes (e.g., "Bay Mir Bistu Sheyn," "And the Angels Sing," "Tzena Tzena") became international hits. But only one ever made it to the top forty in American rock and roll: "Ich Hub Dikh Tsufil Lib" (Yiddish for "I Love You Much Too Much"). Originally written for the Yiddish actress Luba Kadison (1907–2006) by Alexander Olshanetsky (1892–1946), with lyrics by Chaim Tauber (1901–1972), the song was recorded by many internationally known singers—including Seymour Rechtzeit, who sang it in Yiddish, and Connie Francis, Dean Martin, and Ella Fitzgerald, who sang it in English. But the rock and roll version was recorded as an instrumental ballad by Carlos Santana in 1981 on the top-ten album *Zebop!*

Of all the various venues (resorts, social clubs, vaudeville, movie theaters) available between the turn of the twentieth century and the early 1940s, the Yiddish theater provided the klezmer with the most steady work and pay outside of playing weddings and bar mitsves. Yiddish theater in New York City, Boston, Philadelphia, and Chicago attracted thousands of theatergoers. To be hired in New York City the klezmer had to belong to the Progressive Musicians Union (formed in 1890), which was folded into the American Federation of Musicians in 1923. As working-class Jews became more and more politicized because of their daily economic struggles, unions became an important place for artists to seek redress for work-related problems. The unions also provided a place where they could meet and socialize, discuss common problems, and hold their own events. Composers and conductors belonged to the Idishn Muzik Farband (Jewish Music Union), while other employees of the Yiddish theaters belonged to the United Hebrew Trades, and Yiddish actors to the Hebrew Actors Union. Despite being in a new country, playing for the Yiddish theater, on the radio, or in the Catskills a klezmer artist still dealt with a great deal of negativity. So much so that many second-generation American-born Jews rarely heard the term klezmer while growing up—Jewish musicians consciously replaced it with other, more American and more professional-sounding names. When I asked several American-born children of immigrants if they had heard klezmer music in their home while growing up or if their parents ever spoke to them about the Jewish wedding music of Eastern Europe, the replies were typically these:

> My father or any of the other musicians never called it klezmer music. It was just Jewish music. In fact the term klezmer was pejorative. The ranking of the musicians was as follows: the lowest was the *yardnik* [Yiddish-English for "street musician"],who played on the streets and in the courtyards for donations. Then there was the klezmer who could play, but never got a job playing in a theatre or society gig because he couldn't read music.

Then there was the *muzikant* [Yiddish for "musician"] who not only could read music but played several kinds of music. I was a muzikant, a studied musician.[6]

My uncle and his sons played Jewish dance music at all the family *simkhes* [Yiddish for "celebrations"] but I never heard him use the word klezmer to describe himself or his sons. In fact my uncle always said quite proudly he was a *kunstler*, an artist that played Jewish *freylekhs*, Jewish dance music.[7]

We never called this music in our home. To us it was just Jewish wedding music, freylekhs. My mother once told me a story about a Jewish musician from her town who played the violin with his band at all the Jewish weddings; he was blind and played by ear and none of the other Jewish musicians read music either. To me a klezmer was a kind of amateur musician, one who did not have any formal training, a *gimpler* (Yiddish for "one who plays tunelessly") of sorts, who if you asked him to play Bach would just give you a blank look as if you were crazy. One did not study in the conservatory to play Jewish wedding music.

The music we had for the Yiddish theatre in Edmonton while I was growing up was just called Jewish music. If there was dancing involved with the music we called it Yiddish wedding music. Some of it was obviously klezmer, but I really wasn't aware of calling this music anything but Yiddish wedding music until I went to a concert here in Los Angeles where they called the music performed klezmer.[8]

Having said this, there were those, such as Leonard Nimoy, who grew up calling it klezmer and had no negative memories of the music or of the musicians.

My father had a barbershop about a block away from our apartment in the neighborhood called West End in Boston. At home there was some Jewish music but not a lot. We had some Yiddish recordings by people like Seymour Rechtzeit and Moishe Oysher. However there was a group of klezmer musicians who lived in our neighborhood. These were people who did not necessarily make a living from it, but played it well. One of the musicians was a clarinetist named Bass, who owned Bass Beauty Parlor. My first memory of klezmer music was of Bass playing for this fundraiser at our synagogue. There was this party where women raised their hands as they gave donations of one and two dollars for the synagogue. The master of ceremonies would say: "Oh, here comes Mrs. Rosenberg, play klezmers, something for Mrs. Rosenberg." So while they played she marched up with great dignity and dropped her dollar in the bowl. When she turned around to walk back to her table the klezmer musicians played another little piece for her. The music was timed perfectly so that when she got to her seat it ended with a *bum . . . bum . . . bum . . . buuum!*

I also heard klezmer music at family affairs. My father's uncle was a terrific musician and he had four sons who all played instruments. One son was Buzzy Drootin, who went on to play with some pretty good jazz bands.[9] They played at all the family weddings, *bar mitsves*, etc. All I can remember was they had clarinet, piano, and drums in the band. The music was great, like home music to me, and never carried any kind of negative connotation for me. In fact I enjoyed it so much I took up the clarinet for a short period of time. However it was pretty clear I didn't have a natural talent or certainly wasn't obsessed about it. I quickly gave it up.[10]

By the 1930s the first-generation American-born Jews were growing up—a transitional American Jewish culture. The klezmer in Eastern Europe belonged to a community that was much more insulated against encroachment of the gentile world. In the United States things were different. The Jewish immigrant had never experienced a real democracy, where the more one assimilated into American culture, the better were the chances to be accepted. And the use of Yiddish helped to clearly define the Jewish experience for the early immigrants. For the Orthodox Jews, exclusively using Yiddish in all aspects of daily life helped insulate them from the gentile nonkosher world. For the secular Yiddishists, it helped define them politically, socially, and culturally. But for the majority of the modestly religious and cultural immigrants, speaking only Yiddish was a major stumbling block in the process of becoming American. Consequently, thousands of Jewish immigrants went to day and night schools to learn English. With less Yiddish being spoken (and fewer Yiddish-speaking immigrants arriving), there was less need for that nostalgic connection to the old country. This in turn reduced the number of Jewish cafés, restaurants, social clubs, Yiddish theaters, traditional Jewish weddings, and other celebrations that wanted klezmer entertainment. Then the Great Depression began in 1929, and there was less money to hire klezmer musicians, buy recordings, and produce klezmer on the radio.

The final death knell for klezmer music for most Jews in America came after World War II. The Yiddish world was in turmoil. With the destruction of nearly 90 percent of East European Jewry, the spigot that had supplied American Yiddish-speaking communities with fond memories, opportunities to exchange cultural ideas in the arts, and letters and visits from families and friends was all but shut off. Many survivors felt guilty, as did a good portion of American Jewry, for not being able to do much for their brethren during the war. Yiddish culture reminded these immigrants and their children of a world that they wanted to forget because it hurt too much to remember. They now needed to identify not with a ghetto culture perceived as weak and victimized but with a fresh, vibrant, Hebrew culture. After the War of Independence (1948), in which Israel defeated the surrounding Arab countries, Jews throughout the world were proud to be Jewish again and felt they had an independent homeland of their own—a homeland where the Israeli Jew could be religious, secular, or everything in between without being pressured to assimilate into the gentile world. American Jewry looked to Zionism and the fledgling Israeli culture to create a new Jewish consciousness, one that emphasized hope, endurance, and the future. Klezmer music was thus no longer the attractive, inspiring music it had once been. The klezmer's repertoire at Jewish events in the 1950s now included mostly popular American tunes, with only some of the Israeli material and even less klezmer.

Though the heyday of klezmer had already passed by the 1950s, a significant core of immigrant Jews (mostly in the New York region) still enjoyed listening to the Yiddish repertoire. Most of these Jews were either Holocaust survivors, Khasidim, or secular Yiddishists. Thus the more famous klezmer musicians (all clarinetists) like Dave Tarras, the Epstein Brothers, Marty Levitt, and Shloimke "Sam" Beckerman (1883–1974) were able to keep relatively busy by playing for the Khasidim, in the

Catskills, and in the new emerging Jewish market in south Florida for the transplanted Jewish northerners.

There was another Jewish klezmer, a great clarinetist, who lived not in New York City but in Los Angeles and who became as well, if not better, known to Jews and non-Jews than the previously mentioned klezmer clarinetists. This was Mickey Katz (1909–1985). His Jewish recordings sold more than any other at that time and were listened to by many of the klezmer bale-kulturniks and their parents in the 1950s and '60s, thus helping to maintain a link between those who came of age with klezmer prior to the Holocaust and the post-Holocaust generation. Mickey Katz was able to play his style of Jewish music into the mid-1960s, even though most klezmer musicians had retired a decade earlier. Many said disparagingly that Mickey Katz "only" played Jewish novelty music and it was never really klezmer, but nothing could be further from the truth. His two instrumental albums, *The Family Danced* and *Mickey Katz Plays Music for Weddings, Bar Mitvehs and Brisses*, show "his true genius as a bandleader, composer and musician. His band's arrangements by Nat Farber are also works of subversive vision prefiguring Radical Jewish Culture."[11] In truth, his arrangements were innovative and his lyrics jocular and acerbic. However some klezmer purists called Katz's art *shund* (Yiddish for "literary trash") because he dared to make people laugh and, in particular, laugh at their Jewish identity through his parodies of American popular songs in English, Yiddish, and Yinglish.[12]

Jazz clarinetist Don Byron, who played klezmer for the Klezmer Conservatory Band for several years was so moved by some of Katz's recordings that he recorded *Don Byron Plays the Music of Mickey Katz*. Comparing Katz to the late jazz composer and saxophonist Rahsaan Roland Kirk, Byron defends Katz by remarking, "They figure if you're funny you're not serious."[13]

For most of the musicians in the mid-1970s to the early 1980s, playing klezmer music was not a true revival—a stirring up of religious faith among those who had been indifferent—but rather a return to a specific kind of cultural milieu, the one in which either their parents or grandparents had grown up. These bale-kulturniks recreated a specific kind of klezmer music that existed in East European Jewish culture during the mid-nineteenth century through the eve of World War II. They played music that was found in the few klezmer manuscripts and on the earliest 78-rpm recordings.

In the twentieth century there have been five different generations—five waves, so to speak—of klezmer music in America. The first two were the historical and musical mentors for the three bal-kulturnik generations. The first-generation klezmer musicians were those born and trained in Eastern Europe before World War II. Some of them immigrated to America, while others never left. Some of these include Ben Bayzler, Shloimke Beckerman, Naftuli Brandwein, Avram Bughuci, Jerimiah Hescheles, Leopold Kozlowski, Nikolai Radu, Abe Schwartz, Leon Schwartz, Misha Demitro Tsiganoff, and Dave Tarras.

The second generation came to America from Eastern Europe as young children or were American born. They actively played and recorded klezmer music from the

1920s to the early '60s. Their repertoire still included tunes of the first generation, but they also began to combine elements of swing with their klezmer melodies. Some of these musicians were Sid Beckerman, the Epstein Brothers, Mickey Katz, Howie Leess, Marty Levitt, Sammy and Ray Musiker, and Paul Pincus.

The third-generation musicians were the first bale-kulturniks who began playing klezmer in the 1970s. They learned both from recordings and firsthand from those first- and second-generation klezmer musicians who were still alive. Some in the third generation include Michael Alpert, Lauren Brody, Stu Brotman, Marty Confurius, Giora Feidman, Zev Feldman, Barry Fisher, David Julian Grey, Lev Lieberman, Ken Maltz, Zalman Mlotek, Hankus Netsky, Henry Sapoznik, Andy Statman, and Josh Waletsky.

The fourth-generation bale-kulturniks were those who began playing klezmer in the 1980s. They learned equally from the three previous generations, but by the late '80s they began to push the boundaries. Klezmer bands began to experiment with elements from jazz, rock and roll, and ethnic genres like Roma, Balkan, and Arabic music. The establishment of KlezKamp in 1984 in the Catskills became a kind of one-week seminar of sorts for bale-kulturniks and second-generation klezmers to meet, learn, play, and exchange musical ideas with one another. By the late 1980s, Western Europe (particularly Germany) was becoming more receptive to the growing interest in Yiddish culture and brought several klezmer bands from America to tour. The overwhelmingly positive reception these musicians received from critics, audiences, and record companies in Europe convinced some to either base much of their performing in Europe or to completely relocate there. Some of these musicians are Fred Benedetti, Alan Bern, Kurt Bjorling, David Buchbinder, Ismail Butera, Don Byron, Bob Cohen, Adrienne Cooper, Jack Falk, Dave Hofstra, Josh Horowitz, David Krakauer, Margo Leverett, David Licht, Lori Lippitz, Frank London, Wendy Marcus, Jeff Pekarek, Joel Rubin, Lorin Sklamberg, Peter Stan, Deborah Strauss, Yale Strom, Alicia Svigals, Gerry Tenny, and Jeff Warschauer.

The fifth-generation bale-kulturniks are those musicians who began playing klezmer in the 1990s. There is a now sixth-generation—those who began in the twenty-first century (some having first been exposed to klezmer at KlezKamp). Both the fifth and sixth generations continue to forge ahead into the twenty-first century. Many of these musicians came of age in the 1980s, '90s, and 2000s and learned the repertoire not only from the old recordings by the first- and second-generation klezmer musicians but from the cassettes and compact discs of the third- and fourth-generation bale-kulturniks. Another resource, outside of recordings and klezmer music books, which were barely available for the previous bale-kulturniks, was the various Yiddish and klezmer festivals that began in America, Europe, and in the former Soviet Union. The disintegration of the former Eastern Bloc and Soviet Union caused many Jews to emigrate, and many came to the United States. Among these Jews were a number of klezmer musicians (like relics from pre-WWII Jewish life) including klezmer clarinetist German Goldenshteyn (1934–2006) who was born in Otaci, Moldova. He immigrated in 1994 to the United States and brought an infusion of klezmer tunes he learned in Moldova and his own original melodies that few in America had ever heard. Goldenshteyn became a mentor for many klezmer musicians in the fourth, fifth, and sixth generations. He was a kind of first-generation klezmer in that he lived the majority of his life in Eastern Europe and was playing in a style and a repertoire that had not changed since the mid-nineteenth century. In addition to this, several documentary films had become important for many musicians' klezmer education. Though at one time klezmer was only heard at a Jewish wedding in the synagogue courtyard, today it can be heard in venues from Carnegie Hall to the Montreal Jazz Festival.

It is not a coincidence that various bale-kulturniks across the world returned to the music of their grandparents at the same time in the 1970s and '80s. All had come from a positive Jewish upbringing, whether religious, secular, or a combination of both. Some of these musicians' parents were part of the American folk music movement that began in the mid-1950s. The liberal wing of this movement helped galvanize many people, including progressive Jews, to take control of their lives and fight for economic, social, and political justice after the searing McCarthy years. The growing diversity of the country and the rise of the African American and Chicano movements shattered assimilationist theories and encouraged other ethnic groups to slowly begin to research and extol their own unique cultures. Some sociologists say that this examination and proclamation of individual heritages and histories went into high gear with the tremendously popular success of the book (1976) and television series (1977) *Roots* by Alex Haley.

Consequently many young Ashkenazic Jews (second- and third-generation Jews) began to examine and rediscover their East European roots. Some felt disillusioned about the political situation in Israel and turned to their Yiddish roots as an alternative. Others were tired of the focus of East European Jewish history and culture on migration, pogroms, and the Holocaust, and sought more positive aspects. Still others were completely assimilated; for them, returning to Judaism down prescribed religious paths was not an option. Finally, many Jews who were brought up in homes that were devoid of any Jewish spirituality, or whose Hebrew school/synagogue experience left them apathetic, found religious consolation in a return to their Yiddish East European roots. Although many of these same disillusioned Jews wandered off searching for some kind of spiritual fulfillment in other religions and cults, others returned to Judaism through klezmer. Learning to play klezmer was often less intimidating than learning Hebrew or studying the Torah; and going to klezmer concerts was often easier than going to the synagogue. This revival caused a reawakening in the Sephardic world as well. The music of the "fiddler on the roof" that once echoed throughout the Yiddish world of Eastern Europe has pushed many bale-kulturniks to professionally extol the virtues of Jewish culture and religion as rabbis, cantors, teachers, professors, writers, filmmakers, musicians, composers, etc. Klezmer is the sound track of this astounding renaissance.

NOTES

1. Interview with Aaron Penner (originally from New York City) in San Diego, California, May 1, 1981.

2. James Benjamin Loeffler, *A Gilgul Fun a Nign: Jewish Musicians in New York City, 1881–1945* (Harvard Judaica Collection Student Reseach Papers, No. 3 Harvard College Library, Cambridge, 1997), 17.

3. The phrase Borscht Belt was supposedly coined by *Variety* editor Abel Green; it comprised all the Jewish hotel and bungalow resorts in the Catskill Mountains just north of New York City. The Yinglish word *toomler* comes from the Yiddish *tuml*, which means noise, din, racket.

4. Interview with Marty Levitt (originally from Brooklyn) on October 25, 2001.

5. The author coined the term *bale-kulturnik*, as one who returns to his culture and transmits it to others.

6. Interview with Marty Levitt, see note 4.

7. Interview with Nosson Zilberzweig (originally from Bibrka, Ukraine) in Brooklyn, New York, on November 29, 1982.

8. Interview with film director Arthur Hiller (originally from Edmonton, Saskatchewan) in Los Angeles, California, on October 30, 2000.

9. Benjamin Buzzy Drootin (1920–2000) was born in Kiev, Ukraine, and came to Boston in 1924. His father, Leonard Nimoy's great-uncle, had been a klezmer clarinetist along with his two sons in Czarist Russia. Drootin began playing the drums as a teenager; from 1947 to 1951 he was the house drummer at Eddie Condon's in New York. Eventually he performed with many famous jazz musicians, including Wingy Manone, Jack Teagarden, Jimmy McPartland, and Tommy Dorsey.

10. Interview with actor-director-photographer Leonard Nimoy (originally from Boston) in Los Angeles, California, on November 1, 2000.

11. Seth Rogovoy, *The Essential Klezmer: A Music Lover's Guide to Jewish Roots and Soul Music, from the Old World to the Jazz Age to the Downtown Avant-Garde* (Chapel Hill, NC: Algonquin Books, 2000), 189.

12. Yinglish is the combination of Yiddish and English words, e.g., *bouchick, alrightnik, nogoodnik, yardnik.*

13. Josh Kun, *The Most Mishige: The Music and Comedy of Mickey Katz,* unpublished manuscript, p. 6.

3

Accordion

Peter Stan

I would like to share a little about the background that prepared me for a life devoted to my music career as a professional accordionist. My parents are Roma, originally from the Banat region of Serbia, which shares a border with western Romania and southeastern Hungary. It is a region rich in diversity with Romanians, Serbs, Hungarians, Roma, Germans, Krashovans, Ukrainians, Slovaks, Czechs, Croats, and other ethnicities. My brothers and I grew up speaking Romanian in the house. My parents spoke Romani only when they didn't want us to understand their conversations. My parents and my oldest brother left Serbia (then Yugoslavia under the reign of the dictator Josip Tito) and went to Italy before I was born. After living in Italy for almost two years they went by ship to Melbourne, Australia, where my younger brother and I were born. I lived there until I was nine years old.

Music was always a part of our household. Between my dad, my brothers, and me there was always someone playing music in the house. My dad is what you would call an amateur Balkan village musician. Most village musicians could play several instruments, some better than others. My dad played the accordion and a few other wind instruments (flute, ocarina, etc.), and he also sang. My father told us how he wished he could have owned a chromatic accordion as a child, but his family could not afford to buy him one, so I remember my dad ordering his first chromatic accordion (Dallape) from an accordion company in Italy. He waited months to receive it. When his fancy chromatic Dallape finally arrived, he practiced for hours. He used some strange "old school" practice techniques that he had seen in his village, like putting rubber bands and weights on his fingers. I remember once he went to perform for a Balkan wedding, which was the first time he used his accordion. The wedding began in the afternoon and lasted until 6 a.m. the next day. He came home obviously quite tired, set his accordion down, and then proceeded to take all of this money stuffed in his pockets out. I had never seen so much money before. It is customary at many Balkan celebrations to put money on top of the accordion or in the bellows as a tip to the accordionist, a custom I still appreciate. (Ha, ha.)

When we moved from Australia to the United States we met most of my mother's side of the family and friends that immigrated earlier from the Balkans. Everyone spoke Romani, Romanian, and Serbian, and many played music. Eventually I began to learn Romani and Serbian from my family, friends, and the musicians with whom I worked. There were Roma parties at least twice a week. Sometimes the party lasted two days in a row, and the most important part was the music. The people enjoyed the food and drink, but if the music was not good the people did not enjoy themselves. Even with bad food and great music the party was a success.

Once my dad's nephew Pikula Stan came to play the accordion for a Roma party; nobody expected much of him because no one really knew he could play. His playing shocked everyone. His tone, bellow control, and ornamentation were so clean, and he had amazing finger technique. He had an amazing effective light touch to the accordion keys. Pikula had a particular love for the sound of Balkan violin playing. He somehow was able to transfer this beautiful violin timbre and imitate it on the accordion. Immediately after witnessing Pikula playing the accordion I fell in love with the instrument. Pikula became my first teacher. About a year later, he went back to Serbia, and it was impossible to keep in contact with him. Then a few years after that the Balkan Roma accordionist Sinisha Luka returned to New York after living in California. He is still today a superb accordionist. He has a very unusual fingering that enables him to get a specific touch for playing the ornaments. When I was a child just beginning to play the accordion, Sinisha had an answer for everything about playing the accordion. Learning from him was like taking university-level classes from an accordion maestro. I learned a tremendous amount about what the accordion could sound like and how having a specific "touch" to the keys was the linchpin of good accordion playing.

My dad insisted I go to music school so I could learn to read music and know music theory. I am grateful I listened to him. I began playing professionally at various Balkan events when I was seventeen. For the next seven years my focus was on improving my Balkan music playing. Then at twenty-four, I got a call to play for my first klezmer gig. The leader of the ensemble was the wonderful clarinetist, composer, and arranger Harold Seletsky. He brought a lot of klezmer music for me to sight-read. Unfortunately, my sight-reading was not strong then. I was so upset at what I had gotten myself into, I could not wait for the gig to finish. So when we started playing I depended more on my ear and felt that if I adopted my Romanian style of playing, it would get me through the gig. At the end of the gig Harold surprisingly told me he really liked what I was doing and wanted me to join his band, Harold Seletsky and the West End Klezmorim. The ensemble consisted of Seletsky (clarinet), Mary Feinsinger (vocals), Barry Mitterhoff (mandolin, guitar, banjo), Don Butterfield (tuba), Ellis Burger (drums), and myself on accordion. I felt that adopting certain Romanian and Roma licks worked well with the klezmer music, especially the klezmer tunes that either came from Romania or were influenced by Romanian folk music. Playing a klezmer *zhok*, *onga*, hora, or *doyne* was not too difficult to learn. Although I am not a purist in the playing style of klezmer, I learned a lot over the years having played many klezmer gigs and finally joining Yale Strom & Hot Pstromi. Yale has always encouraged me to add my Balkan and Roma influences into my accordion playing. It is difficult to say what the exact style of klezmer accordion playing was 150 years ago, because we have no sound recordings.

Our knowledge of the accordion playing in klezmer ensembles comes from the few 78 LPs that we have from the turn of the twentieth century to the end of the 1920s. One can however surmise that the accordion was being used in klezmer ensembles as early as the mid-eighteenth century in parts of Transylvania, the Banat, and even up through the Carpathian Mountains because we have evidence from photos of Roma playing the accordion in these regions, and many Roma played in klezmer ensembles led by Jews. One of the Jewish musicians to have left his mark in playing klezmer accordion was Gregori Matusewitch, who was from Minsk, Belarus. He was primarily a classical musician, but like other klezmer musicians of the nineteenth century he played longer compositions that combined both classical and klezmer musical idioms. Matusewitch followed in the footsteps of some famous klezmer musicians and composers who played both classical and klezmer: Joseph Michael Guzikow, xylophone (also known as the *hackbrett* in Yiddish), from Sklov, Belarus (1806–1837); Avron Moshe Khorodenko, more famously known as Pedotser from Berditshev, Ukraine (1828–1902); and Alter from Tshudnov from Cudniv, Ukraine (1846–1912). Matusewitch played with a broad smooth tone. "Indeed a characteristic of Matusewitch's 'folk' style was his frequent use of a warbling fast trill using the upper third. When playing klezmer tunes, he made ample use of vocalistic escape tones . . . known as *krekhts* in Yiddish, appoggiaturas, trills and occasional syncopation."[1]

Another early klezmer accordionist was Max Yankowitz. Yankowitz's style really imitates the voice one traditionally heard singing Yiddish folk songs and synagogue prayers. In his tune "Az Du Furst Avek" (Yiddish for "As You Travel Away"), recorded in 1913 on the Columbia label, you hear the smooth, more legato fingering and very light use of the bellows. All of the ornamentations are executed rather softly. Another thing that struck me listening to several of his recordings is the sparse use of the left-hand bass. It is the *tsimbl* that doubles the bass line or sometimes plays it entirely alone. "The fact that Yankowitz used the bass so sparsely was the first indication that his instrument may have been a 3-row chromatic right hand with a push-pull left-hand system, as it would have been difficult, though not impossible, to have continuously doubled some of the fast moving bass lines of the tsimbl with the graceful right-hand phrasing Yankowitz displays."[2]

One accordionist who was a great musician and probably played closest to what we consider the "true" klezmer accordion style was Mishka Tsiganoff, who was a Kalderash Roma born in Odessa, Ukraine. He immigrated to America sometime around World War I and lived in Manhattan and Brooklyn. He spoke fluent Yiddish (like Yale Strom Roma informant from Chisinau, Nikolai Radu) and performed with some of the great klezmer and Yiddish vocalists during the 1920s and '30s. Some of these artists were Molly Picon, David Medoff, Moishe Oysher, and Dave Tarras. In fact Sy Tarras, the youngest son of Dave Tarras, remembers Tsiganoff coming to his home in Brooklyn with Molly Picon for a visit on several occasions.³ In the few archival recordings that I heard Tsiganoff's technique, the ornamentation, trills, and his left-hand control created a balanced, clean sound. Unlike Yanowitz, he played with more of an attack with each note. His execution was clearer and had more punch, and he seemed to play at a higher level of proficiency than Yankowitz.

Despite the misconception among some klezmer musicians today, the accordion has been a part of the tradition from at least the latter part of the nineteenth century. Often one hears on early ethnic recordings (Greek, Turkish, Serbian, Romanian, Roma, and klezmer) the accordionist accompanying the vocalist. Many people think that Yiddish folk singing is not part of the klezmer genre, but this is incorrect. The tradition of singing klezmer, like the *batkhn* before and during a Jewish wedding, goes back at least to the sixteenth century. It was the vocalizations the batkhn sang that informed the accompanying instrumentalists of how to use certain klezmer ornamentations. Through the immigrant era (1881–1924) to the klezmer revival years (1975–1990), the accordion has been a vital part of many klezmer ensembles. The concert that really lit the fuse for the klezmer revival was the November 1978 Dave Tarras reunion concert produced by the Balkan Arts Center that included Andy Statman (clarinet) and Zev Feldman (tsimbl). Joining Tarras were his longtime bandmates Irving Graetz on drums and Sammy Beckerman on accordion. On Tarras's last album recorded in 1979, one hears a rhythmically steady accordion by Beckerman, but it is rarely in the foreground. He accompanies the clarinet with a solid but light touch. Occasionally you hear the accordion doubling the melody, but rarely do you hear the accordion taking a solo. This was typical of most klezmer accordion playing: reliable, accurate playing heard in the background. However, since the revival of klezmer, the accordion is often a featured soloist, like the clarinet and violin.

I realized that a large repertoire of klezmer music has been influenced by Romanian folk music the first time I performed with Harold Seletsky and the West End Klezmorim. Harold handed me a sheet of music that said "Doina in G Minor." As I began to play I immediately recognized the doyne (Yiddish spelling) form. The definition of a doyne is a sweet rubato expressive song that can be sad or happy. There are many musical terms in Romanian folk music that are also used in klezmer, such as doyne, hora, *sirba*, etc. And much of this klezmer music from Romania has been influenced by Turkey and the former Ottoman Empire. Klezmer musicians in Romania (Wallachia and Moldavia) often traveled back and forth from Constantinople (Istanbul, Turkey). Many Phanariote Greeks (originating from the Greek neighborhood in Constantinople called Phanar) were brought by the Ottoman Turks to work as civil servants and merchants. They left an indelible mark on these provinces of Romania and especially in the folk music. The itinerant klezmers would meet these Greeks and play for and with them, as well as exchange tunes with each other. Some klezmer ornamentation like the krekhts can be heard throughout Balkan music. There is a *ketsev tants* (Yiddish for "butcher's dance") melody I play with Hot Pstromi that is very similar to a Greek *Hasapiko*, thus there was constant borrowing and sharing among musicians bringing different styles to klezmer in Romania at least as far back as the eighteenth century.

However, years ago I was hired for a gig by a wonderful musician but a klezmer purist. Before I even started playing he came up to me and told me that the accordion should be used only for accompaniment and to not add any fancy playing or fills. All he wanted from me were straight chords. There are certainly occasions when some accordionists play too much and get in the way. With the Banat style of Balkan music I grew up playing, oftentimes the accordion is the main melodic instrument even while accompanying, and it can be intrusive in not letting the other instruments sing.

Some of my best learning experiences through the years have been playing with musicians that played at a higher musical level than I was capable of at that time. One of those gigs was in 1985, when a Romanian band (vocals, violin, cimbalom) came to perform in a small nightclub, and they needed an accordionist to perform with them. They were all superb musicians, and I was learning on the job. The new repertoire, the guidance, and the constructive criticism they gave me really made me grow as a musician.

Then there was the time I was hired to play with an ensemble called The Golden Land Orchestra at the famous Russian Tea Room. All of the musicians were excellent: reeds, three violinists, piano, contrabass, and me on accordion. There were many times when it came to my solo part and I played something very difficult and technical even though it didn't groove with what everyone else was playing. If I had played my solo much more simply and focused on tone, it would have been better. Their soli often had fewer notes but were much more beautiful and sweeter than what I had played. A few artistic, expressive, musical notes can often say much more than many notes played in solo. No matter what style you are playing, there is always an artistic way to interpret the music. You must first know what you want to hear coming out of your instrument and how to express this feeling. This is done through finger control, bellow control, and your ability to execute this on your instrument.

The best way for the accordionist to set his/her dynamic levels is to listen to the lowest-sounding instrument in the band and make sure it can be heard while you are playing. At the same time, you need to make sure there is enough support for the solo instruments, for the vocalist, and for the audience to feel the beat and groove. For example, let's say you are going to accompany a vocalist, violinist, clarinetist, etc. (with or without a band), and there is no arrangement. Instead of just concentrating on your playing, focus as well on supporting the soloist and making sure you complement the performance. When there is no specific arrangement, often the singer or soloist will explain what they want from the accompanist. An accompanist must be flexible. For example, the singer might say: "Play only chord accompaniment in section A, only improvised fills in section B, and double the melody occasionally playing harmony in section C."

I have accompanied klezmer and Balkan vocalists that wanted me to play a constant melody line while they sang, while others have wanted the opposite: they did not want any melody line from me. As an accompanist you must learn how to naturally feel what should be played while backing the soloist before adding harmony, melody, and fills. Onstage anything can happen, and you should be prepared for the unexpected. A solo might be thrown to you when you are not expecting it, a different rhythmic groove might be thrown into the middle of the song, or you might even have to transpose to a different key that you weren't expecting.

There is an art to being an accordionist in a band that performs for parties. The main hora dance set at a wedding or *barl bas mitzve* is a vital part of the celebration. This could go on for as long as an hour with no breaks. As a klezmer accordionist you need to have a large repertoire of dance tunes memorized and be able to change keys immediately, especially when playing the hora set. It is very often the accordionist that sets the tempi, keeps the energy driving and people dancing because the instrument if played properly can be dynamically loud and rhythmically forceful. As long as the rhythm is moving you can add some improvisation to each dance tune. Some dance tunes at these Jewish celebrations have lyrics to them, but most do not, and all the people care about is the driving rhythm, especially if you are not playing with a drummer. I have seen virtuoso musicians that, when they perform at weddings and other celebrations, are not able to connect with the folks in the party, whether they are dancing or not. The food may be bad at a wedding, but this will not be remembered if the music is hot. It is the music that creates the life of the party. A bad band will be remembered long after the event is over.

When we hear the word *technique* we sometimes interpret this to mean the ability to play fast notes. However, to have really good technique on your accordion, playing fast notes is the least of it. What is important is having good finger movement and control of each note, passage, and phrase played. You have to have the same strength and stamina in each finger, and perform with the same dexterity from the beginning to the end of the piece. As an accordionist, you need to have complete control of your touch on the keys, finger phrasing, and bellow work whether you are playing legato, staccato, martillato, etc. If you play such virtuosic pieces as "Perpetual Motion" by Paganini or "Flight of the Bumblebee" by Rimsky-Korsakov, you have to play it clean and at a fast tempo, but you also need to bring out the story of the song. "Az Der Rebe Elimelekh" (Yiddish for "As Rabbi Elimelekh") is an example of an easy Yiddish folk song, but again, each note squeezed out of the bellows must express sorrow and joy.

Producing a good tone is a large part of playing the accordion. You want a warm, sweet, full sound as opposed to a thin, weak, or squeaky sound. Playing loud doesn't mean you're playing a good tone on your instrument. Everyone also has his/her own tone character that represents him or her, and even when there is more than one accordionist playing in an ensemble you should be capable of creating your own unique tone. For me, tone is produced not only through the ability you have for playing the instrument but is heavily influenced by your personality and what is in your mind and heart.

The groove in which you play has a few definitions (rhythmic patterns, harmonic patterns, melodic patterns), which are basically different musical components that build a cohesive sound. A solo melody has its own particular groove. It is the way one note meets and then talks to the next note in a specific rhythmic pattern, phrase, or pulse. Whenever a clarinetist or violinist takes a solo (for example, while playing a *freylekhs*), the rhythmic groove accompanying each of them will have its own personal characteristics. As an accordion player, my rhythmic groove changes each time a different musician is playing, even if it is the same solo in terms of notes. Each musician brings something unique to their sound, and you have to accompany accordingly. If the soloist and band are not grooving together, then the solo will sound boring.

EMBELLISHMENTS

Playing with klezmer ornamentation is important and helps identify the genre of music you are playing. Playing with mordents, trills, slurs, krekhts, pralltrills, bended notes (*tshoks*), and glissandi bring out the tune's life, warmth, and singular personality. Still, today among folk musicians in the Balkans, there really is no name for each specific embellishment. Many musicians in the Balkans still use the word *triller*, which defines all ornamentation. There are amazing self-taught "old school" accordionists that are not aware of how they create such a beautiful tone, with amazing ornaments, and are not able to explain how they do it. It's as if it is just the natural way of playing the instrument. The best system of learning Balkan and klezmer phrasing and ornaments is through playing with the actual musicians that play the style or by listening to recordings and learning by ear. This book will be a great guide for learning how to play klezmer, but remember, you will need to put in extra work by listening and analyzing klezmer recordings. I suggest you listen to the few archival recordings we have of Mishka Ziganoff and to these contemporary klezmer accordionists: Ismael Butera, Patrick Farrell, Joshua Horowitz, Sy Kushner, as well as myself. Another aid that will help you is to listen to some recordings of famous Romanian accordionists, such as the legendary Marcel Budala. Listen closely to how they adapt their ornamentation to each tune. An ornament written down in notation form looks the same to everyone but can be interpreted in different ways by each musician. Embellishments should come naturally, in places you are not aware you are adding them once you are familiar with the music. I have had the wonderful pleasure of meeting, getting to know, and listening to some of the best Roma Balkan accordionists in the world (Ionica Minune from Bucharest, Perica Jovanovic-Gula from Serbia, and Lelo Nika from Malmo, Sweden), who each play their embellishments differently from each other.

Here are two examples of how a simple ornament can have different interpretations when executed. Figure 3.1 is the most common ornament. This is used when trying to imitate a Yiddish song or klezmer melody. These are questions you need to ask yourself when trying to execute this ornament: Is the first note played legato or staccato? As the B♭ joins it, is it hit legato or staccato? What is the rhythmic pulse between the first notes? What is the rhythmic pulse when you combine everything together?

Example 1: Bar #10 of ODESSA BULGAR

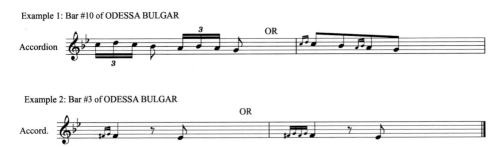

Example 2: Bar #3 of ODESSA BULGAR

Figure 3.1   Examples of mordents as executed in "Odessa Bulgar."

Figure 3.2 is a list of some basic ornaments for the accordion, with additional ornaments shown in figures 3.3 and 3.4. I would rather not call each by any specific name, since I grew up learning that ornaments are not something added to a tune but are already implied in the melody line. The krekhts is the key ornament in klezmer music. When executing this ornament, as shown in figure 3.5, the C note is barely heard or pressed. As you can see, a blink of a second can change the whole character in execution. You must listen attentively when trying to copy a style (phrasing, accent, pulse).

EMBELLISHMENT #1: MORDENT

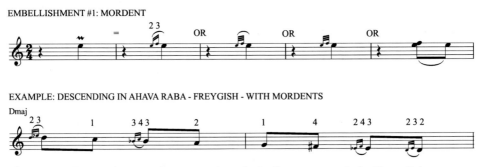

EXAMPLE: DESCENDING IN AHAVA RABA - FREYGISH - WITH MORDENTS

Figure 3.2   Four variant mordent executions, including an example in Ahava Raba with fingerings.

EMBELLISHMENT #2: INVERTED MORDENT

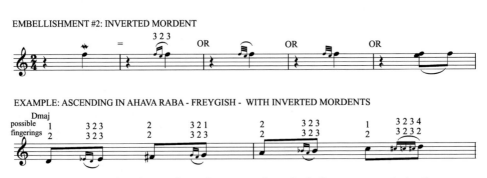

EXAMPLE: ASCENDING IN AHAVA RABA - FREYGISH - WITH INVERTED MORDENTS

Figure 3.3   Four variant inverted mordent executions, including an example in Ahava Raba with fingerings.

EMBELLISHMENT #3: PRALLTRILLER

EXAMPLE: DESCENDING IN MISHEBEYRAKH WITH MORDENTS WITH THE PRALLTRILLER

Figure 3.4   Pralltriller mordent execution, including an example in Mishebeyrakh with fingerings.

EMBELLISHMENT #4: KREKHTS

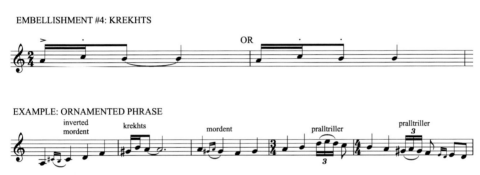

EXAMPLE: ORNAMENTED PHRASE

Figure 3.5   Krechts execution, with an example of a fully ornamented phrase.

When you practice it should always be about results—not about how many hours you spend on any one exercise. When I really got serious about playing the accordion as a kid, I used to say to myself, "I must practice six to eight hours every day." Now I say it is better to have an effective practice session than just banging out the hours. There are people that practice for years and do not have much to show for it in terms of being able to play their instrument and being able to play musically. To grow you must try to learn something new each time from the same piece of music you might have played already for twenty years. You have to inspire yourself. Musicians that play the same repertoire, same licks, and same improvisation will become boring to themselves and especially to the audience. Do not let your practicing become a mechanical exercise in which you clock in and out but have not explored something new about the piece you are practicing (technique and theory) and something new about your instrument. While learning to play the accordion, record yourself and analyze your own performance. Taking an ear training class can also be very beneficial. The more you can learn by ear and distinguish the ornamentation by ear will make you a much stronger player.

Here are two questions that you will need to answer when you record yourself: Is the rhythmic pulse in the left hand too choppy, too sluggish, or perhaps overpowering the right-hand melody? How does your finger-touch combined with the control of the bellows sound in respect to playing the rhythm that is required? Be sure each note connects with the next. Remember each note should be having its own conversation with the others, which is expressed in the same volume, touch, and pulse. Some experts will say that certain klezmer ornamentation should be only used for specific melodies. I say you should know this and be able to play correctly in the klezmer style but also not be afraid to put a new spin on a traditional piece. This makes it your own. A Jewish hora played by a klezmer from Moinesti, Romania, in 1822, was heard

KLEZMER ENDING ('CODA')

Figure 3.6   A typical klezmer ending.

RIGHT HAND ACCOMPANIMENT PATTERNS

LEFT HAND ACCOMPANIMENT PATTERNS

Figure 3.7   Right- and left-hand accompaniment exercises.

differently and interpreted (even just slightly) differently by a klezmer who played that same hora, from that same town but not in 1922. Music should be understood, felt, and heard as a living organism and not as a fossil.

Improvisation (among many Balkan musicians it is called *taksim*) is putting your exclusive statement into that instrumental melody or song. The first few notes of any improvisation are extremely important. When someone is beginning a speech, the timbre of the voice, the initial first few words can give a clear picture of what the speech is about and its emotional tone. Remember that improvisation will allow you the opportunity to express yourself freely in a spiritual way. Again, it is not the amount of notes played during an improvisational passage but what and how these notes are played. Sometimes just holding one note for eight beats or repeating a phrase as many as ten times can create a beautiful sonic tension that has placed the audience in the palm of your hands. Feel free to explore, but stay in the mode of the particular klezmer tune you are playing. Remember the more you know your instrument, the more it will become an extension of your personality and the more you will master the klezmer style of accordion playing. Like anything in life, if you take the time to plant the seed then take the time to nurture it, you will reach your full potential.

Section B (starting at bar 18) of the Romanian Serba has a few Romanian-style grace notes. To get acquainted with the style, I suggest first practicing the ornament as a double instead of as a grace note. This will help you get the feel. Once you are comfortable with playing the melody like this, start playing the ornaments as grace notes. Try this approach to the first section also.

Figure 3.8 Three klezmer scales, including Ahava Raba played in thirds.

ODESSA BULGAR (Mishka Ziganoff- transcr. Peter Stan)

Figure 3.9 "Odessa Bulgar," classic klezmer accordion piece.

PREPARATION FOR PLAYING ROMANIAN SERBA

Figure 3.10 An exercise to prepare the student to play the Romanian Serba.

ROMANIAN SERBA RHYTHM - cymbalom style

Figure 3.11 An example of Romanian-style accompaniment.

Figure 3.12   Romanian Serba.

2

Figure 3.13　Romanian Serba, continued.

Figure 3.14　Irinina's Waltz, in lead sheet format.

DISCOGRAPHY

Budowitz Ensemble, *Mother Tongue: Music of the 19th Century Klezmorim* (Koch Schwann, 1997).

Goldies Records, *Klassic Klezmer* (3 CD Set) (Intermusic, 2001). Forty-two classic klezmer tunes from the 1920s to 1940s including three by the accordionist Mishka Ziganoff.

Sy Kushner Jewish Music Ensemble, *Klezsqueeze!* (CDBY, 2008).

Yale Strom & Hot Pstromi, *Café Jew Zoo* (Naxos World, 2003). Peter Stan plays on this recording.

NOTES

1. Joshua Horowitz, *The Klezmer Accordion: Old New Worlds (1899–2001)* (Musical Performance, Vol. 3, Parts 2–4, pp. 135–62, 2001), 140.

2. Ibid., 142.

3. Interview with Yale Strom, May 7, 2012 (on the telephone from San Diego). See his book *Dave Tarras: The King of Klezmer* (Kfar Sava, Israel: Or-Tav Music Publications, 2011).

4

Bass

Jeff Pekarek

I first became interested in folk music in 1972, at the age of fourteen. I was fortunate to be studying the classical bass with the Puerto Rican maestro Federico Silva, and I paid for lessons by busking in Balboa Park (in San Diego, California) with my friends Fred Benedetti and James Sliva. Sliva introduced me to British folk music via the vinyl albums of Fairport Convention and Steeleye Span. In 1974 I began studying with Bertram Turetzky, who instilled in me a deep respect for all music and generally prepared me for life as a professional musician. In 1979, after three years as a contracted member of the San Diego Symphony, I decided to leave classical music and move to Great Britain to learn what I could about the folk music of the British Isles. I subsequently also became interested in Russian folk music and Himalayan music and began to play balalaika as well as bass.

In 1981 I was asked by my high school friend Yale Strom to assist in forming Zmiros, a band to perform klezmer music, and so I began to learn what I could about it. Klezmer was just beginning to enjoy its great revival in the United States, and it was a very exciting time to be involved. In 1988 I helped form The Electrocarpathians, a band that experimented with the fusion of klezmer and other East European styles with "vintage rock" and Latin sounds. This project led me to a great deal of library research, as I explored the common roots of klezmer, belly dance (*raqs sharqi*), and Hungarian (*czardas*) music and possible connections with the polka, especially as it evolved in the Americas in the late nineteenth century. Being a bassist by profession, I was always keen to understand the role and history of the bass in all of these styles.

THE LATE NINETEENTH CENTURY

The bass (contrabass, string bass, double bass) is mentioned often in early literary references to klezmer music, along with the violin and hammered dulcimer (in Yiddish, *tsimbl*). This same trio (violin, hammered dulcimer, and bass), with the addition of accompaniment violas, is also the classic nineteenth-century folk band of the Carpathian region, still heard today in Poland, Hungary, and Transylvanian Romania. Many examples of the traditional music associated with this type of band have been carefully transcribed, a result of the general movement to study and preserve folk music in Central Eastern Europe initiated by Zoltan Kodaly (1882–1967) and carried on by his students and admirers. Some performance practices pertaining to the bass were thus preserved, and since these practices are known to have been common to Polish, Hungarian, and Rom bassists, it seems reasonable to assume that Jewish (and Slovak and Romanian) bassists of the same region and time period would have used the same techniques.

In the Carpathian region a slightly smaller bass (sometimes called a beer-bass, after the inn bar environment) was sometimes used, being easier to carry along small mountain roads. The three-stringed bass (tuned G-D-G) was also used. The bow was of the German (underhand) type. The immediate ancestor of the German bass bow, which was a bit thicker and not concave-arched (the Dragonetti bow), is also seen in some photos. The above-mentioned transcriptions (from the early twentieth century) suggest that the bass was most frequently played *arco* (bowed) in these small violin-driven bands, although pizzicato (string-plucked) is also indicated. In Hungary and Transylvania the *col legno battuto* (string struck with the stick of the bow or a drumstick) technique is known to have been popular. This is perhaps due to the coexistence of the *cordon*, an instrument smaller than the *bier-bass* but larger than the cello, which was played col legno battuto when accompanying the *citera* (a fretted instrument native to Hungary, which is similar to the American mountain dulcimer). In any case, the arco, pizzicato, and col legno battuto techniques are known to have been employed by East European bassists in the nineteenth-century folk music environment, and it can certainly be inferred that the bass was most frequently played with a bow in klezmer bands.

THE EARLY TWENTIETH CENTURY

Commercially produced recordings of klezmer music began appearing in the first decade of the twentieth century. Most examples are from the United States, with old-world specimens appearing after the birth of the Soviet Union. Early recordings of American klezmer orchestras show them to be relatively similar to each other in style and repertoire, at least into the mid-1920s. Yale Strom has commented that this might have been due to pressure from the record labels to record mainly well-known pieces, which would be more likely to sell. This "first generation" of klezmer recordings is a principal source of our modern knowledge and concept of klezmer music, especially as regards the clarinet, brass instruments, flute, and drums. Unfortunately very little bass can be heard on these recordings.

There are also recordings of smaller ensembles from which details regarding the performance practice of violinists, accordionists, and pianists can be gleaned. Especially when playing in these smaller groups, violinists exhibit the archaic, "oriental" ornamentation that is also heard in the Carpathian string bands mentioned above— descending portamenti (slides) and trills and extended mordents (melismata) involving three or four notes, of which two might be separated by a minor third. The contrast in style between the small groups and the orchestras indicates that klezmer music must have evolved considerably as a result of increased access to band (woodwind) instruments, beginning in Czarist Russia and continuing in America. It appears that klezmer was moving toward the global dance orchestra mainstream. In any case, it can be safely assumed that the klezmer orchestra bassist usually played the same part as the tuba or euphonium (the trombone often also played this lowest part but just as frequently was given a tenor voice that might also vary in rhythm). When doing so, the bass would vary only as necessary due to range constraints. This doubling of the bass with the low brass was the norm in all dance orchestras on both sides of the Atlantic. As the orchestrator Philip J. Lang noted: "The string bass is used in the band to color and soften the brass bass, for solo passages (usually pizzicato), and to support the reed bass."[1]

The principal klezmer forms dating from this time period are the *bulgar/freylekhs*, the *sher*, and the *khusidl* (*khasid*), as shown in figures 4.1 through 4.3. In each case the bass generally plays a simple root-fifth line in quarter notes. In the sher, the bass might play eighth notes (usually the arpeggiated chord) in the last bar of a four- or eight-bar phrase. Similarly, in the bulgar, which features a more syncopated drum pattern, the bass might mimic the drum pattern or rhythm of the melody at the ends

Figure 4.1   A typical khusidl root-fifth bass line.

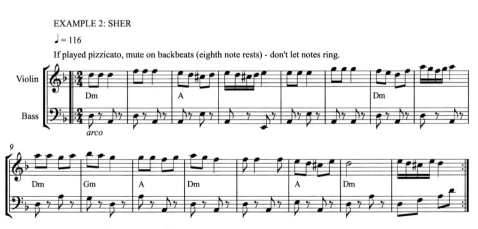

Figure 4.2   A typical sher bass line.

EXAMPLE 3: BULGAR/FREYLAKH

Figure 4.3   Bass line for a complete traditional bulgar/freylekhs, including percussion part for comparison.

of phrases or other exposed situations, but not too frequently, as the British tubaist and bassist Paul Tkachenko has noted.[2] This conservatism has its roots in the need to provide a clear, repetitive rhythm for dancers. In modern times, of course, where klezmer is heard as much in the concert hall as on the dance floor, the bass is freer to play more complex patterns.

Note that in the example of the sher (figure 4.2), the bass plays arco, and execution is clipped (non legato). Although there are no adequate recordings from the period (i.e., recordings in which the contrabass can be discernibly heard), written transcriptions of related music that is similar in rhythm and tempo indicate that this is the authentic performance practice. In addition, one can point to the style and delivery of the *guardia vieja* tango, a genre that is contemporary and similar at least from a rhythm section (drums and bass) perspective.

The bulgar/frcylekhs is the fastest and most common of the three main "old school" klezmer dance styles. As mentioned above, the bass generally does not join in the well-known (and well-loved) syncopated drum pattern but plows forward relatively relentlessly with predictable quarter notes. The concensus among older bassists is that this style is played pizzicato. It seems to me that differences in execution between the sher and the bulgar are generally owed to the difference in tempo.

In this time period we find recordings of the hora that are clearly in 5/16 time (though contemporary printed music always shows it in 3/8). (See figure 4.4.) A good example of this is the recording of "Oriental Hora" by violinist Abe Schwartz (with his daughter Sylvia at the piano), Columbia E4825. The same piece was published by the Kammen Brothers, with the title "Roumanian Horra" [*sic*], in 3/8, which must be considered an inaccurate transcription. The klezmer hora appears to be related to the *paidushka* (Bulgarian for "Limping Girl"), a traditional Bulgarian/Macedonian form[3] that shares the 5/16 time signature and some melodic features, although it is played a bit faster. Today the hora is usually played in 3/8, often with a slightly anticipated third beat that recalls the 5/16 meter. (See figure 4.5.) The 3/8 hora has certainly been recorded many, many times and has even found its way into popular perception through movies like *Brighton Beach Memoirs*. Should we consider the hora in 3/8 to be incorrect?

Of course, the older rhythm can be reestablished. Here is a similar case in point: The Serbian/Macedonian folk song "Sano Duso" is in 7/8. In the 1950s, an inaccurate transcription in 3/4 was published and distributed in the United States. By the

Figure 4.4   Bass line for a traditional hora played in 5/16.

EXAMPLE 5: ROUMANIAN HORRA

Figure 4.5 Typical bass line for a traditional hora.

1960s, with direct communication between Yugoslavia and the United States at a low point, many American musicians were performing the song in 3/4. However, the folk dance revival of the '80s corrected the trend, and today with easily accessed references on the Internet, it's almost unthinkable that a professional musician would perform it in the wrong rhythm. Still, as concerns the klezmer hora, perhaps it is best for the bassist to be ready to play the hora both ways.

Early twentieth-century klezmer bands also played waltzes, polkas, and the *kozatshok/kozatzke* (in Ukrainian: *hopak*). Their treatment of these styles conforms to contemporary standards.

THE MID-TWENTIETH CENTURY

From the late 1920s onward, as the technology of recording continued to improve, records and movie sound tracks captured more of the bassist's art, so we have more concrete evidence of how the instrument was used. Klezmer music, like all other styles, was increasingly exposed to popular mainstream influences. In both America and Europe, Jewish music grew in breadth and sophistication, although this process was effectively halted in Europe during the Holocaust.

In the United States, Broadway theater music may have furthered some clarification and enrichment of klezmer's harmonic language, both directly and through the interaction of composers, arrangers, and pit musicians with the Yiddish-language (Second Avenue) theater scene. The V9, Vb9, IIm7b5, VIm7 (in major key), and VI7 (in minor key) chords appear in this time period. The songs of Molly Picon are excellent examples of this trend. For instance, "Yidl Mit'n Fidl" (Abraham Ellstein, 1936) features root movement of a tritone in the introduction, a theatrical device already common in transitional incidental music, used to evoke the passage of time or space and also to distract the audience from moving set pieces. The same song features a descending chromatic line in the midrange that creates the progression Im-Im7-IVm6; where the traditional klezmer chord changes would more likely have been Im-I7-IVm.

There were several non-Jewish styles that exerted some influence on klezmer music through the '30s and '40s, the most important being swing and tango. Swing's quick triplet rhythms had no parallel in traditional klezmer music, but its broad melodic palette easily found room for klezmer scales and ornamentation, and evidence of klezmer influence on swing abounds. Conversely, the introduction of characteristics of swing into klezmer music probably owed much to the efforts of composer/arranger Sam Medoff (bandleader of WHN's radio show *Yiddish Melodies in Swing*), beginning around 1937. Swing influence on klezmer is evidenced by "walking" bass lines in some up-tempo environments, like the recessional in figure 4.6.

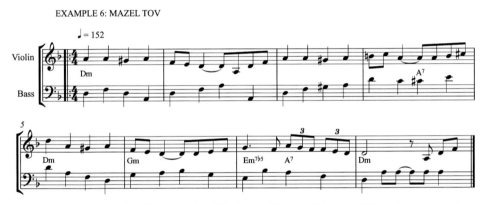

Figure 4.6   **An example of a swing (walking) bass line used for a traditional recessional.**

Buenos Aires was the center of a large Yiddish theater scene in the '30s and '40s, and perhaps this is why there is some tango influence discernable in klezmer music. Deborah Davis, soprano and expert on the work of Molly Picon, has commented that, according to her research, significant numbers of Yiddish theater artists migrated seasonally between New York's Second Avenue scene and Buenos Aires, following the work. Interestingly, the tango bassist uses the bow in many situations, and the klezmer bassist, quite comfortable with the bow, may have more readily adopted tangoisms than, say, the swing bassist. It should also be noted that the tango profoundly influenced Romanian popular music in this period. (See figure 4.7.)

It can be said that the klezmer artist who absorbed the most influences and produced the most "fusion" in this time period was the great Mickey Katz, likely because comedy gave him an excellent vehicle for doing so. One cannot go wrong imitating the playing of the great session bassists (like Larry Breen) who backed him up.

Figure 4.7   An example of a tango bass line used for a vocal piece.

Terkisher is a klezmer form that derives elements from Turkish, Greek, and Lebanese sources. As Paul Tkachenko has noted, the various Turkish *cifteteli* bass patterns can be employed, as well as other belly-dance rhythms. (See figure 4.8.)

Figure 4.8 An example of a typical cifteteli bass line.

THE LATE TWENTIETH CENTURY AND THE REVIVAL

In the 1950s and '60s, Israeli music seemed to be steering clear of klezmer music. This was actually a trend that started decades earlier and was fueled by the desire to define and establish a new musical culture. Israeli composers rarely referenced klezmer music in their works, looking instead to the music of other East Mediterranean countries, global pop trends, and Jewish liturgical music.

This began to change in the '70s, however, and increasing migration from Russia and the Ukraine in the '80s and '90s led to a more benign attitude toward klezmer and other aspects of Yiddish culture. Some examples of klezmer/Israeli fusion can be found in the music of the Ukrainian/Israeli composer Vladimir Shainskiy. Most known for his music for children's songs in Russian, he also composed Jewish liturgical music that has distinct klezmer characteristics, and pop songs so widely recognized in the Russian-speaking world that they are considered traditional music. Bass lines in Shainskiy's music tend to work on classical voice-leading principles. Similarly, many modern klezmer bass players who were conservatory trained in Russia and the Ukraine in the '60s, '70s, and '80s use classical voice-leading in bass lines.

TOWARD THE FUTURE

Throughout the second half of the twentieth century, Bertram Turetzky worked ceaselessly to make the bass a pillar of the avant-garde. He taught extended techniques like the "seagull" (repeating harmonic portamento) to hundreds of bassists and influenced the entire profession. As Turetzky himself has demonstrated, many of the colors explored in his classic manual *The Contemporary Contrabass* lend themselves wonderfully to klezmer music, especially slower-tempo pieces, where the bass is more exposed.

Figure 4.9 **Bass line for a complete traditional kozachok, showing classical voice-leading.**

There is a common performance practice in klezmer music that the bass, in playing the long, bowed tones of the *doina*, should delay introducing a chord change until several seconds after the lead instrument has (musically) indicated the new chord (see figure 4.10). This has been mentioned by many contemporary klezmer artists (Pete Sokolow, Robert Zelickman, Strom, and Tkachenko, to name a few). I personally feel that this "delay" applies specifically to *improvised* doinas and should be a natural effect of improvisation, not to be contrived or exaggerated.

Bass   55

EXAMPLE 10: DOINA (IN THE STYLE OF LEOPOLD KOZLOWSKI)

Figure 4.10   Bass line for a non-improvised doina, showing the use of extended techniques.

In the 1990s, several artists worked toward blending Latin and klezmer music, notably Yale Strom, who wrote and recorded many pieces showcasing the talents of Afro-Cuban percussion master Gene "Negro" Perry. This trend continues into the twenty-first century with artists like the Global Shtetl Band (based in Germany), featuring bassist Markus Mueller.

The general movement to explore fusion among traditional folk styles, which began as World Beat in the '80s, has produced literally dozens of hybrids represented by hundreds of bands. The place of the bass in this process has been less than prominent, since it is usually replaced by the (electric) bass guitar. Still, the primacy of the acoustic bass in folk music, along with the unique array of colors that the instrument produces, should guarantee it a place in future exploration. Currently, in bands that play traditional klezmer music, the bass is still greatly preferred over the bass guitar.

DISCOGRAPHY

Mickey Katz (Larry Breen, bass), "Mazel Tov Dances," *Greatest Shticks* (1959).
Zmiros (Mark Dresser, bass), "Beatriz's Nign," *Eclectic Klezz* (1985).
The Electrocarpathians (Jeff Pekarek, bass), "Kamariska," *Fighting for Harmony* (2007).
Margot Leverett (Marty Confurius, bass), "Tumbalalaika," *2nd Ave. Square Dance* (2008).
Global Shtetl Band (Markus Mueller, bass), "Der Alter Nign," *Bist Geven* (2012).

NOTES

1. Philip J. Lang, *Scoring for the Band* (New York: Mills Music, Inc.,1950), 75.
2. Paul Tkachenko, *Klezmer Bass: An Overview*, accessed October 2009, www.tkachenko .co.uk/introtoklezmerbasspaultkachenko.pdf.
3. Boris A. Kremenliev, *Bulgarian-Macedonian Folk Music* (Berkeley: University of California Press, 1952), 112.

5

Clarinet

Norbert Stachel

I'd like to clarify that my goal in writing this chapter is to define my klezmer style of clarinet playing and how I have developed the techniques that work for me. I do not make any claims that my techniques are unique or that they have been handed down to me or that they are the only approach to becoming a proficient klezmer clarinetist. I will say they have worked for me for over thirty-five years, and many of the finest klezmer clarinetists share a good deal of the same techniques that I use. I do not consider myself to be an absolute purist or even an ultimate authority of "klezmer only" clarinet playing. In fact, I am also an active professional player of other woodwinds, including saxophone and flute, in a large variety of American and international musical styles. I often employ klezmer techniques on all of the instruments I play when performing music other than klezmer to create certain sonic effects.

First I will give you a brief history of the klezmer clarinet musicians and how they became a fixture in klezmer music from the mid-nineteenth century through today. Klezmer music was an oral tradition for the majority of klezmer musicians through World War I. The vast majority could not read or write music, so tunes were passed down from one musician to another, from ear to ear. This is one of the main reasons there is so little in the archives today of any music that was printed before the nineteenth century. Notating music among the klezmer musicians did not become the norm until the late nineteenth century, and klezmer ethnomusicological research did not begin until the twentieth century.

Jewish musicians were introduced to the clarinet and brass instruments when they were forced to serve in the Czar's army. Until this time, the common instruments in a Polish klezmer ensemble were the violin, *tsimbl*, and wooden flute. Czar Nicholas I (1825–1855) felt such animosity toward his Jewish subjects that he introduced twenty-five years of mandatory service in the Czarist army. For many Jewish boys from ages twelve to eighteen, before they served in the Czarist army, they were forced into indentured servitude on Russian or Ukrainian farms. At eighteen, if these young

Jewish men had survived this cruel and harsh treatment, they were then sent to the army, where they had to serve twenty-five years. This was Czar Nicholas's plan to help accelerate the process of assimilation among the Jewish population and the eventual disappearance of the Jews. The thought was if there were fewer and fewer eligible Jewish men able to get married, have children, and raise a family, the "Jewish question" would answer itself. This horrible military system of having to serve twenty-five years began in 1827 and ended in 1856. Nearly half of the fourteen thousand boys who served in the Czar's army during these years were forcibly baptized.

The Jewish men who either were klezmer musicians or learned quickly to play an instrument understood that being in the band was a lot safer than being one of the regular soldiers who fought on the front lines. In the Czar's army there was not much opportunity for string players, so many violinists became trumpet players to avoid combat. Other Jewish musicians began playing the brass instruments, and some the woodwinds. Consequently, after playing for many years in the military bands, the Jewish musicians who went back to playing klezmer music after their discharge brought with them their instruments and music knowledge, which in turn influenced the repertoire and makeup of the klezmer bands in Europe and eventually America.

> My grandfather was only eight years old when the *khapers* [Yiddish for "grabbers, catchers") took him away. His parents never saw him again. The khapers took him to some town where he worked as a field hand at a Ukrainian farm. When he was eighteen they put him into the Czarist army. Because he was nice-looking, stood erect, and had a nice beard, they taught him the clarinet so he could play at the officer parties. Being able to play music spared my grandfather the worst of all those military years. One day he was in a town where no Jews were allowed to live but only to pass through. So this Jew met my grandfather and asked him how much longer he had to serve. Then the man said that he had a little daughter and that by the time my grandfather was released from the army his daughter would be marriageable. He told him to go to Konotop. Since my grandfather had no family, when he was honorably discharged from the army he went to Konotop. And he married that young woman, my grandmother.[1]

The klezmer's repertoire was varied in Eastern Europe since he played for Jews and non-Jews. He played everything from a *freylekhs* to a quadrille. The vast majority of the tunes were functional melodies—they were played for dancing at weddings and parties. However, there was a core repertoire of tunes that were just for listening and creating a heightened spiritual religious ambience. Some of these were the *badekns*, *bazetsn*, *doyne*, *terkishe-gebet*, and *zogekhts*. It was during the time when these particular tunes were played that the soloist (often the violinist or clarinetist) would show off his musical skills with a virtuosic performance. And it was during these musical displays that the klezmer clarinetist began to make a name for himself.

One of the first klezmer musicians to have become famous throughout Europe was Mikhl Joseph Guzikov (1806–1837), who played the clarinet at Jewish weddings. However he became famous from playing a Belarusian instrument called the *shtroyfidl* (Yiddish for "straw fiddle"), which was similar to the *hackbrett*, which he modified by increasing its range to two and a half octaves so that it was closer to today's xylophone. He played the shtroyfidl for concerts in large halls across Europe. This portable, rather enigmatic instrument consisted of a set of solid wooden bars tuned diatonically and laid horizontally across a bed of cylindrically wound straw, which created the sound cavity. It was played by striking the bars with small wooden sticks.

The klezmer scene in America during the 1920s through World War II produced four main clarinetists that set the standard for klezmer clarinetists through today: Shloimke Beckerman (1883–1974), Naftule Brandwein (1889–1963), Max Epstein (1912–2000), and David Tarras (1898–1989).

Beckerman was born in Rizish, Ukraine (East Galicia), to a family of klezmer musicians. He came to the United States around 1910. He had great ears and technique and could pick up a style of playing and a melody after having just listened to the tune once. He was one of the early klezmer musicians to easily cross over to jazz and back to klezmer. He appeared regularly as a soloist in the 1920s with the Paul Whiteman Orchestra at New York's Little Club. He played and recorded with Abe Schwartz in the 1920s. His recording "Tikias Shoyfer Blozn /A Galitzianer Tentsl" became a seminal recording for many revival klezmer musicians in the 1980s.

Max Epstein played saxophone and violin but became famous for his clarinet chops. Born in New York City, he became a professional musician at age twelve when he took a job playing violin to accompany silent movies and cartoons like *Popeye* and *Betty Boop* for the creators Max and Dave Fleischer. Then by the late 1920s Epstein realized that the old-world sounds that the immigrant Jews had been brought up on were now being replaced with the sassier and brassier sounds emanating from the jazz clubs. The violin could not compete, so he learned to play the saxophone and clarinet. Epstein is considered the only American-born klezmer clarinetist equal to European klezmer players like Dave Tarras and Naftule Brandwein. He and his brothers (Isidore, aka "Chi" or "Chizik," 1913–1986, saxophone and clarinet; William "Willie," 1919–1999, trumpet; Julius "Julie," 1926– , drums) worked successfully in New York's Yiddish community during its heyday in the 1930s and '40s. They recorded a classic LP in the 1950s *Dukes of Freilachland*. In the mid-1950s Epstein and his brothers began to play for the *Khasidim*, and this lasted until the early 1990s when they all moved to South Florida. The *bal-kulturnik* scene brought the Epstein Brothers back into the public eye. They started attending KlezKamp in 1991 and were the stars of their own documentary film *A Tickle in the Heart* (1996).

Naftule (sometimes spelled Naftuli) Brandwein's father Peysekh was a famous violinist and *batkhn* (Yiddish for "wedding bard, jester") originally from Przemyslany, Poland. There were ten boys and four daughters from four different wives. All the boys played in the father's klezmer ensemble. Naftule arrived in New York City in 1908 and was a larger-than-life figure who cut a huge swath through the city's venues. He was as famous for his onstage and offstage antics as he was for his clarinet virtuosity. Not at all the shy type, by the late 1920s he had recorded several 78-rpm records with Abe Schwartz and was calling himself "The King of Jewish Music." He played hard and lived hard.

Naftule was supposed to be the *vilde* [Yiddish for "wild one"] *meshugena* [Yiddish for "crazy"] and a bad drinker. Dave (Y.S. Tarras) said: "All of Naftule's friends were bums, gangsters." He hung around in the *kretshmers* [Yiddish for "taverns"] of the Lower East Side like Café Royale and those places. He was well known with the Yiddish actors, and very well known with the underworld crowd, especially Murder Inc. For them he was a real showman.[2]

Julie Epstein remembers Brandwein:

I played with him a couple of times. He was a fine player though I was partial to my brother Maxie's playing. He was more like Tarras than Maxie and played with a choppy style. He was a very, very handy guy and played a lot in the Jewish theatre. However he was a drunkard and a lady's man, a swinger in those days. After a job he'd say to me: "Come swing with me."[3]

Brandwein's on- and offstage antics made it difficult for him to remain with a band, as fellow players grew tired of his histrionics. Thus in 1923, Tarras was offered Brandwein's chair (previously it had been Beckerman's chair) after he was fired by Joseph Cherniavsky (Yiddishe American Jazz Band) in Philadelphia.[4] After the Philadelphia job Cherniavsky offered a weeklong job in the Bronx to the young Dave Tarras, paying him $110. Tarras thought to himself:

When I heard $100 I nearly fainted, so I accepted and saw that I can make a living here. I went to my brother-in-law [Max Shapiro] and his two partners in the furriers and said: "Thank you very much for giving me a job. I'm quitting."[5]

Dave Tarras was born in Ternovka, Russia (Ternivka, Ukraine), and came from a long line of klezmer musicians. Tarras's first instruments were the flute, mandolin, *cobza*, guitar, and balalaika, which he learned to play from his father. At thirteen he switched to clarinet, having taken just three weeks of lessons from a klezmer in Uman. Upon his return home, Tarras's father had him join an ensemble playing at a gentile wedding. His father was impressed by his son's tone and encouraged him to only focus on the clarinet. I wager that if he had had him focus on any of the plectrum instruments he was playing (and still played for himself throughout his life), the klezmer revival scene might be a bit different today with some talented cobza and balalaika players fronting klezmer bands.

Tarras arrived in New York City in 1921. After a short stint working at a furrier's, Tarras began to focus only on playing klezmer music in 1923. His ability to transpose and sight-read music (something Brandwein could not do) and his no-nonsense personality made Tarras the go-to guy for many Jewish ensembles. He worked with most of all of the top Jewish bandleaders of the 1920s and '30s: Joseph Rumshinsky, Abe Ellstein, Alexander Olshanetsky, Al Glaser, etc. He also became the go-to guy for many of the popular Yiddish singers and composers, which kept Tarras busy in the recording studio. Some of these folks were: Aaron Lebedeff, Moishe Oysher, Molly Picon, Seymour Rechzeit, the Barry Sisters, Sholom Secunda and many others. Along with his Jewish records Tarras also recorded Greek, Polish, and Russian tunes.

Like Max Epstein, Tarras lived long enough to become a music icon during the initial years of the klezmer revival. Klezmer musicians, enthusiasts, and journalists beat a path to Tarras's apartment in the Coney Island neighborhood in Brooklyn to sit and listen to this great musician. With the help of Andy Statman (clarinet/mandolin), who became Tarras's protégé, and Zev Feldman (tsimbl and ethnomusicologist), Tarras went back into the recording studio one last time in 1978 with the trio he had played with for over thirty years, with Irving Graetz on drums and Sammy Beckerman on accordion. The record *Dave Tarras: Master of the Jewish Clarinet* is now considered a classic in the klezmer oeuvres.

The musician who knew Tarras probably better than anyone other than family and started playing with him in 1959 until Tarras passed away in 1989 was Pete Sokolow (b. 1940). Sokolow was a vital klezmer link between the generation of Tarras/Brandwein and the klezmer *bale-kulturniks* of the mid-1970s through the '90s. Sokolow started with the piano, but by age thirteen his idol was Benny Goodman, and he fell in love with jazz (particularly Dixieland) so he began to learn the clarinet; by age fifteen he was playing tenor saxophone as well.

> I probably first heard about Dave in the mid-'50s when I started taking up the clarinet and saxophone. He was "king of Jewish clarinet playing at that time" even before I heard of Naftule Brandwein. Then when I heard Naftule Brandwein on a recording, I wanted to meet him and hear him live. It was in 1957 and I was playing in a hotel in the Catskills and he was only a mile away playing at Shloyme Erinreich's hotel, an orthodox hotel. I just couldn't get anybody to drive me. I would have loved to have met Naftule because Naftule was something else! He was supposed to be the *vilde* but Dave was totally a different kind of guy.[6]

Then in 1959, Sokolow was booked to play with Tarras's band at the Hotel Astor. "I was scared to death. I was going to meet and play with the king of klezmer. So Tarras walks in and looks me up and down and says: 'I am teacher of clarinet. All the best players come to me.' In other words, get down on the floor and bow down. Ironically however, he didn't play the clarinet and any bulgars on that job. He played 'Sheyn vi di Levune' [Yiddish for 'As Beautiful as the Moon'] and those kind of tunes. The biggest problem was we had a three saxophone section and he was playing tenor saxophone and I was playing alto. He was God-awful on the saxophone."[7]

It was natural that some kind of rivalry existed between Tarras and Brandwein. Some say it was started by the side musicians who played with each of these superb clarinetists, and other say there was no rivalry between the two, but this perception was started by the *bale-kulturniks* to help them define their own particular klezmer clarinet style. They wanted to differentiate themselves from other klezmer clarinetists and create a following among the public—those who liked the Tarras style of playing versus those who liked the Brandwein style more. Julie Epstein recalls his first time meeting Tarras:

I was maybe sixteen or seventeen and I was watching my brothers play at this catering hall where just down the hallway in another room Dave was playing. I already knew who he was from the radio. He was the number one Jewish clarinetist in New York. Then when I was about twenty, twenty-one, I played with Dave at a catering hall. The first thing I remember was Dave telling me: "*shashtil* [Yiddish for 'shh, quiet'] not too loud." And the second and last time I played with him he said the same thing: "*shashtil* shut-up and play soft." He was a great player but aloof. His style was very European. He played with a quiver, a shaky kind of sound like a machine gun while Maxie played smoother, American style.[8]

His brother Max Epstein recalls:

My idol was Dave Tarras but he played like a cold fish. His technique was classical and he played wonderfully. But the one who played with fire, who ripped your heart out of your body, was Naftule Brandwein.[9]

Andy Statman recalls:

Dave always told me he respected Naftule and they never had any kind of rivalry between themselves. Naftule was not classically trained and loved Greek and Turkish music. His sound reflected this and you could say he played just on that fine line between rough and out of control. Dave loved classical music and was so proud of his siblings that played professionally in the Soviet Union. I think he regretted a little that he was not able to go further with his classical studies. He studied with Simeon Bellison[10] who was the principal clarinetist for the New York Philharmonic and one of the major classical clarinetists who played the Albert system like Dave. Dave would often warm up playing classical etudes and you can hear these influences in his improvisations and compositions.[11]

Finally, Pete Sokolow recalls:

Naftule was very interested in Middle Eastern kind of stuff. His thing was he liked Greek and Turkish music very much. And he played the Turkish melodies. He was really into that Eastern roughness. He often played very fast with all kinds of trills, glissandos, and jumps and he'd turn his back to the crowd so if there happened to be another clarinetist in the room he couldn't copy his fingerings. Naftule's timbre immediately twisted your ear, it was an important part of his style, whereas Dave favored a more violin kind of approach, a bit classical in its delivery with a *khazonish* [Yiddish for "cantorial"] quality. And he liked the major minor *freygish* [Yiddish for "mode similar to Phyrigian"] European modes. He liked Hungarian fiddle pieces very, very much. Things that Dave played were smoother so he liked the repertoire that was in the Kostokowsky book. Dave liked the more Russian, Polish and Hungarian, Romanian a lot of things having to do with the *kretshmer* music they played. Both of them played other instruments. Naftule's original was trumpet before clarinet so his attack was moreta, ta, ta, ta while Dave played some flute before clarinet and his attack was much smoother. His playing struck a responsive chord in the next generation of people. And there was nothing that he did that was not immediately taken up by other people. His style was much more accessible to the ears of the American Jews who were born here and especially to those who were assimilating.

He really had the *loshn* [Yiddish for "language"]. As soon as Dave came around, everyone forgot Shloimke Beckerman and Naftule Brandwein. Shloimke played more *neyekh, neyekh, neyekh* attacking the notes then biting them off while Dave did less of that and relied more on portamento and cantorial phrasing.[12]

The klezmer clarinetist has been a fixture in klezmer music in America since the first klezmer recording "Belfs Romania Orchestra" to have the clarinet in the ensemble (two violins, piano, and clarinet). It was released in 1913. From that time through today, other klezmer clarinetists besides the big four—Beckerman, Brandwein, Epstein, and Tarras—left a legacy of wonderful klezmer recordings. These clarinetists were born in America and straddled both the immigrant and revival eras. They were: Marty Levitt (1931–2008), Howie Leess (1920–2003), Mickey Katz (1909–1985), Paul Pincus (1918–2005), Rudy Tepel (1917–2008), and still going strong Ray Muziker (1922–). And since the mid-1970s, there have been a number of clarinetists around the world that have made their mark on the revival klezmer scene, but I will only mention those in America: David Julian Grey, Ken Maltz, David Krakauer, Margo Leverett, Andy Statman, and up-and-comer Michael Winograd, as well as myself.

When I was young, I started developing an ear and understanding of Ashkenazic music from growing up in a home steeped in Russian and Polish Jewish culture, where the lingua franca was Yiddish. My mother was a survivor of the Minsk Ghetto and had life experiences very close to those portrayed in the modern film *Defiance*, including living and working several years in the forest outside of Minsk while hiding from the Nazis. Before she went to the partisans, she hid for three months in a gentile family's cellar in Minsk before the ghetto was liquidated. My father was a Polish survivor who fought with the Polish Jewish partisans then later in a battalion of partisans under the command of the Soviet army. He reached the rank of captain, riding horseback in the Soviet cavalry fighting fascism and racism.

Growing up I listened to my parents and their close friends singing songs in Yiddish, Russian, and Polish during frequent social gatherings. Many were songs of the Jewish resistance, partisan songs from World War II, as well as Russian and Polish folk songs and popular classics from before and after the Holocaust. Such songs were permanently ingrained into my psyche, for example, "Oyfn Pripetshok," "Papirosen," and "Ochichornia," along with some classic Mickey Katz recordings played regularly in the house. Katz played great klezmer clarinet but did not always get the same praise as Brandwein or Tarras because he was known as a musical parodist rather than just a straight klezmer musician. This all led to my familiarity and interest in playing the clarinet and klezmer music.

In my adolescence and early teens I discovered a local band, The Klezmorim, who later became leaders in the world klezmer revival movement. Over the next several years, I became friends of musicians in the band, and in 1985 they asked me to join the band. However the invitation conflicted with an offer to join, record, and tour with the Sheila E. band (which was opening up for Prince) and then tour with Lionel Ritchie, so I turned down The Klezmorim's offer. When I returned to San Francisco, I continued playing music, especially klezmer, with other groups in the Bay Area.

The most important component of learning how to play any particular style of music well and "authentically," is immersing yourself into the music to such a degree that it feels like it's entering into your bones and flowing into your bloodstream. This is the only way to prepare yourself to feel the true essence of the music and appreciate its vibrancy. After all, folk music such as klezmer is a living testament to the history and collective emotional experiences of that culture and its people. It has been passed down from one generation to the next; and that transcends any professor's attempt to mechanically and coldly "explain" in a theoretical way the essence of Ashkenazic music.

The two klezmer clarinetists that have really shaped my playing were Naftule Brandwein and Dave Tarras. I listened to their recordings extensively, and I learned a tremendous amount from both players. As I stated earlier, both were virtuosi and quite different from each other, with Brandwein's style sounding very emotional and aggressive in an old-world style and Tarras seeming more polished and innovative. I strongly suggest students should play along with recordings of these two masters the best they can, transcribing their favorite songs on their own accord or looking for published transcriptions. I found a personal connection to the style and music of Naftule Brandwein. This is because Brandwein was from the same area in Galicia (Lviv, Ukraine, region) as my father and his family, and his playing was so emotionally deep. In comparing the two styles of the aforementioned masters, I found that Brandwein tended to play very aggressively in his rhythmic approach, played with very precise tonguing, and used klezmer ornamentation skillfully and tastefully. Tarras, on the other hand, was impeccably accurate, clean, and polished in his clarinet performance. On many recordings, Tarras liked to make use of the broad sound of his low register on the clarinet. Like a great classical music virtuoso, it seemed like he never made a mistake! However, it is Brandwein's playing that brings tears of both joy and melancholy to my eyes every time I hear him.

I have chosen Brandwein's "Nifty's Eigene," which was recorded in 1922 and Tarras's "Branas Hassene" recorded in 1941 to compare their similarities and differences. Both tunes are played in the same key, mode, and tempo. Both players played with a strong tone and plenty of klezmer nuances in their ornamentation. Brandwein played with a "bouncier" rhythm and an exaggerated staccato feel, and he took quite a bit more chances with very intricate ornamentation, using his signature mordents and false fingerings. Tarras's tone had a smoother feel and seemed to "play it safe," sticking to the more typical ornamentation, mainly using trills instead of the mordents favored by Brandwein.

The following explanation is for those musicians who are already somewhat proficient on the clarinet, with a working understanding of and a reasonable ability to play the instrument dynamically and in tune:

Much as with jazz, a klezmer clarinetist must develop the skills of improvising and intuitively know how to blend, harmonize, play a supportive role, and solo in any type of ensemble situation. To develop these skills, the student must have a practice regimen including extensive ear training in order to quickly and easily call and respond to the music as it is being played in real time. The klezmer must be able to quickly determine in real time what key and mode the song is based in and be able to follow the chord movement as it is happening. This includes spending quality time in the practice regimen learning and memorizing all of the scales, arpeggios, and modes used in klezmer music in all twelve keys.

The clarinet does have its own unique set of physical characteristics that make it easier to play in certain keys. Mastering breath techniques is vital for the student to be able to use specific ornamentation that gives klezmer its unique expressive sound. The two key ornaments that create the clarinet klezmer sound are the *krekht* (which sounds like a laugh) and the *kneytsh* (staccato note bursts using a combination of the diaphragm and the tongue).

I find it difficult to play klezmer modes on the B♭ clarinet in certain keys that are often favored by violin and accordion players. For me, the difficult (concert-pitched) keys are B, E, A, E♭, A♭, D♭, and G♭. My favorite concert-pitched keys to play klezmer on the B♭ clarinet are F, C, D, and G.

Tone color is a very important factor in playing klezmer clarinet. In my opinion, a jazz tone can be similar to a klezmer tone. When I play both klezmer and jazz, I use a looser embouchure, compared to a tighter embouchure when I play classical music. I also take slightly more mouthpiece in my mouth when playing klezmer, compared to a smaller bite when I play classical music. For klezmer I use a mouthpiece with a larger tip opening, combined with a softer reed. The range of mouthpiece tip openings that I use for klezmer measure from .050 to .060, combined with a number 3-strength reed. Using this setup and embouchure approach, the player will achieve more volume and a more aggressive and lively tonal palette better suited for klezmer.

Vibrato and note bending are also very important factors in achieving a natural klezmer sound. In jazz, bending *up* to a note is common—this achieves a sort of "bluesy" effect. I use this technique somewhat sparingly when playing klezmer, however. When playing klezmer music, I more often bend *down* to a note from a passing note above the desired melodic note for a "sighing" affect. When I play klezmer, my vibrato on the clarinet is a fast, but shallow and narrow vibrato. When the musician combines these note-bending techniques with dynamic volume swells, decrescendos, and vibrato, he or she can ultimately achieve very emotional musical phrases and passages that can evoke deep feelings in both the player and the listener.

Probably the most used ornamentation among klezmer clarinetists is the vocal emulation technique—the previously mentioned krekht. However some aspiring musicians may think that if they learn how to krekht on clarinet, they now are full-fledged klezmers. If you do your listening homework, you will find that on recordings by Brandwein and Tarras the krekht is rarely heard. I play the krekht by doing fast, simultaneous breath (diaphragm) and jaw releases without the use of tonguing in the upper register, descending on a scale either chromatically or on a specific passage of a melody I am learning. Be careful, because overusing the krekht is inappropriate and irritating musically, and the musician is creating a parody of the music. Instead, I often use the kneytsh, which can be done more subtly and stylishly when combined with grace notes and note bending.

Other important techniques I use on clarinet in klezmer music are the implementation of other ornaments when playing the melody or improvising. These ornaments are: grace notes, trills, tremelos, mordents, glissandos, and certain note combinations ("licks" or "riffs," to borrow some jazz terms) that are commonly used in the klezmer idiom. One example of a typical common "lick" would be playing the following notes in the key of C on B♭ clarinet: E D♭ C D♭ E F G. To give this note sequence more color ornamentally, I would insert the notes E and D♭ played as fast grace notes passing in between the first D♭ and the following C. Note that this mode is based off the fifth mode of the so-called Hungarian minor or harmonic minor scale in the key of F Minor. It's even sometimes referred to as the Jewish scale. The complete scale of the fifth mode of the F minor Jewish scale is: C D♭ E F G A♭ B C. If you tastefully combine some of the ornaments along with a nice warm vibrato, some note-bending techniques, and volume swells, with a carefully placed krekht and a graceful kneytsh for good measure, you will start getting the idea of what is possible in achieving an expressive klezmer playing style.

Like classical music, there are those in the klezmer world who feel that the genre needs to be kept to the traditional repertoire. I agree that klezmer students should learn the traditional repertoire and be able to play it with great proficiency. Playing the traditional tunes preserves and extols the past. However, once you have learned the traditional tunes, you must explore what other musical worlds you can take klezmer to. Like jazz, I believe that klezmer music deserves to continue to evolve while still retaining its soul, essence, and roots. Klezmer should not be preserved as a museum piece but should have the opportunity to reach forward to explore new ideas and territories harmonically, rhythmically, and melodically in order to stay fresh and exciting. Klezmer has always been a genre of folk music that changes with the times, places, and people who play it. It is a music that borrows and blends with music from other cultures. The klezmer repertoire in Halberstadt, Germany, in 1468 was certainly not the same repertoire played by the klezmer musicians in Minsk in 1868. This is how the music stays alive and interesting for future generations to enjoy and explore.

In addition to practicing the scales and musical examples I have given, one must listen to some of the classic klezmer recordings listed below. I encourage the student of klezmer to listen, analyze, and compare recordings of klezmer clarinet styles with clarinet recordings of Turkish, Greek, Armenian, Bulgarian, Serbian, Moldavian, and Macedonian clarinet styles to understand where and how the style developed and evolved over the years and how these styles influenced the klezmer musicians in all these regions.

The klezmer clarinet style is unique, though closely related in form and style to the folk and traditional music from the aforementioned Eastern European and Near Eastern countries. For me, the klezmer style has its own identity because of the bittersweet, brooding, melancholy, humorous emotions that are so soulfully alive in the melodies and improvisations. The essence of Jewish prayer, longing, reflection, and spiritual devotion reach out to me when I open my soul to klezmer music.

DER HEYSER BULGAR

Figure 5.1 "Der Heyser Bulgar," a traditional bulgar/freylekhs.

Figure 5.2   Classic klezmer hora.

Doina No. 1

Dave Tarras
arr. Jeff Pekarek and Yale Strom

Figure 5.3   A doyne by Dave Tarras.

Figure 5.3   A doyne by Dave Tarras, continued.

Figure 5.3 A doyne by Dave Tarras, continued.

Here is a list of some of my favorite klezmer clarinet recordings, including one of myself playing, for you to enjoy and learn from.

1. Naftule Brandwein, "Wie Bist Die Gewesen Vor Prohi" (track 9, *King of the Klezmer Clarinet*, 1922)
2. Naftule Brandwein, "Freilicher Yontov" (track 25, *King of the Klezmer Clarinet*, 1922)
3. Naftule Brandwein, "Vie Tsvie Is Naftule Der Drite" (track 24, *King of the Klezmer Clarinet*, 1922)
4. Naftule Brandwein, "Heiser Bulgar" (track 1, *King of the Klezmer Clarinet*, 1922)
5. Dave Tarras, "Chusen Kala Mazel Tov"
6. Andy Statman, "Maggid" (track 1, *Between Heaven & Earth*, 1997)
7. Naftule Brandwein, *King of the Klezmer Clarinet* (Rounder CD, 1997)
8. Dave Tarras, *Master of Klezmer Music, Vol. 1, 1929–1949* (Global Village CD, 1995)
9. Norbert Stachel, *The Absolutely Complete Introduction to Klezmer* (tracks 6, 13, 20, 21, 27, 29) (Transcontinental Music, 2006)

NOTES

1. Yale Strom, *The Book of Klezmer: The History, The Music, The Folklore from the 14th century to the 21st* (Chicago: A Cappella Books, 2002), 95.
2. Yale Strom, *Dave Tarras: The King of Klezmer* (Kfar Sava, Israel: Or-Tav Music Publications, 2010), 18.
3. Ibid.
4. Joseph Cherniavsky (1894–1959) the cellist, bandleader, and composer was born in Lubny, Ukraine. As a young boy he was trained as a klezmer, left the klezmer for classical music and returned as an adult to klezmer and Yiddish song. Cherniavsky's grandfather was purported to have been the real-life prototype for Sholom Aleichem's klezmer Stempenyu (1822–1879), who he wrote about in his novella by the same name originally published in his *Folksbibliotek*, adapted in 1905 for the play *Jewish Daughters*. Educated at the St. Petersburg Conservatory, he was a student of Alexander Glazounov Rimsky-Korsakov. After immigrating to New York, Cherniavsky began an association with Maurice Schwartz and his Yiddish Art Theatre. The first team-work's production was Cherniavsky's play *Moyshe Der Fiddler* produced by Schwartz. Their biggest hit working together was Shloyme An-ski's popular play *The Dybbuk*, first performed on September 1, 1921. In 1922, Cherniavsky established the Yiddishe American Jazz Band. The band took a traditional klezmer lineup and blended it with modern American dance styles such as the fox-trot. The band toured the American and Jewish vaudeville circuit extensively. Some of the ensemble members were Cherniavsky on cello and his wife Dora (Lara) on piano, Naftule Brandwein (later replaced by Dave Tarras), and Shloimke (Sam) Beckerman on clarinet. In the late 1920s Cherniavsky moved to Hollywood, where he wrote the musical score for several films including *Show Boat* in 1929. He toured the United States as a conductor in theaters and in concerts. He also created and conducted the NBC Radio program *Musical Camera* in New York.

5. Strom, *Dave Tarras: The King of Klezmer*, 18.

6. Ibid., 31.

7. Ibid., 32.

8. Ibid.

9. Joel Rubin, *Im Zentrum eines alten Rituals: Die Klarinette in der Klemzer-Musik* (Munich/Berlin: Prestel Verlag/Musikinstrumenten-Museum, 2004), 9.

10. Simeon Bellison, a clarinet virtuoso, was born in Moscow on September 4, 1881. He showed musical talent at an early age and began studying the clarinet at age nine with his father, who was a klezmer. A year later, he played in the Voluntary Fireman's Band, which his father conducted, and in several military bands. Many klezmer musicians who performed at weddings and dances also played in the Porzhone Komande—Fireman's Brigade, an ensemble that played for special community celebrations and at parades. In 1902 Bellison organized the Moscow Quintet and gave a series of concerts throughout Russia, Poland, and Latvia. In 1918, when musical activities were at a standstill in Russia, he organized a second ensemble in St. Petersburg. He named the group Zimro (meaning "singer")—a group of six musicians featuring string quartet, clarinet, and piano—and formed the ensemble in order to support the creation of the state of Palestine and to collect funds for a music conservatory in Jerusalem, and under the flag of the Russian Zionist Organization, Zimro started a pilgrimage throughout the world. During its three years of activity, the ensemble played in the Urals, Altay, all the large Siberian cities, China, Japan, India, Canada, and the United States. It was in 1919, while Prokofiev was living in New York waiting for the premiere of *The Love for Three Oranges*, that this small group of Jewish musicians, former schoolmates from the St. Petersburg Conservatory, approached him with the idea of writing a piece for Zimro. Zimro had by then toured for three years, arriving in America in 1919. They decided to commission a work by Sergei Prokofiev as they knew this would give their ensemble's mission more prestige. As they wished the work to have a Jewish cast to it, Bellison gave him a notebook of Jewish folk songs. Prokofiev, who never worked with folk material, was not enamored with the project but finally composed it in one evening. The composition was his "Overture on Hebrew Themes for Clarinet, String Quartet and Piano Op. 34." It premiered in New York City on January 26, 1920. Bellison was engaged as first clarinetist of the New York Philharmonic Symphony Orchestra from 1920 until 1948.

11. Strom, *Dave Tarras: The King of Klezmer*, 44.

12. Ibid., 22.

6

Drums

David Licht

Before I begin to tell you the history of percussion in klezmer, I would like to thank Yale (my Motown homeboy) for asking me to write this chapter. I haven't revisited the classic klezmer 78 LPs with headphones since the late 1980s. Though the catalog of early klezmer recordings is limited in number, each title is an essential piece of the treasure trove of klezmer that was recorded before World War II. An era I like to think of as the "golden era" of American klezmer. Thanks to archivists Henry Sapoznik, Michael Schlessinger, Kurt Bjorling, Martin Schwartz, and Joel Rubin (to name a few), we have the collections of music from Schwartz, Kandel, Belf, Beckerman, Tarras, Brandwein, and many others to enjoy and learn from. After twenty-nine years, since I first heard the Folkways (now Smithsonian/Folkways) recording *Klezmer Music 1910–1924* while I was playing with the band Shockabilly a year before moving to New York, I am still trying to get inside the heads of some of the great klezmer drummers of the past. Put on a cassette, a CD, an LP, or your iPad with closed-ear headphones, shut your eyes, and enter the time machine and imagine you are in the room with these incredible musicians. Then listen a second time to the same melodies, and this time try tapping out the rhythms and singing the melodies.

My approach to klezmer drumming reflects my approach to any music: shape the songs with rhythm and melody. Enhance each song, provide strong support rhythmically, and highlight the melody. The drummer's role in a klezmer band depends on that band's instrumentation. Does the ensemble use a full drum set or just a *poyk* (Yiddish for "drum"), which was the traditional set up for drummers in the mid-nineteenth century through World War I? The poyk could be either just a tom-tom and cymbal or bass drum and cymbal.

The original snare drum was the medieval tabor from fourteeth-century Europe, although the basic concept is a small double-headed drum with a single wire (snare) stretched across the bottom head for a higher-pitched resonance. This usually accompanied a three-hole flute similar to a fife for folk music and dance events. This musical arrangement soon progressed to military events, used both to relay signals and to accompany marches. The bass drum was predated by a pair of kettledrums used to accompany warriors in fourteeth-century Persia. The poyk came directly from the military bass drum with a cymbal mounted on top. The cymbal can be traced back to Greece in the fourth century BCE. Eventually the separate snare drum and cymbal were played simultaneously by one person marching in the military band.

How and at what level the drummer plays dynamics is crucial. The drum set can easily drown out most acoustic bands. Once a sound system is being used, you are in the hands of the engineer, but stage volume is still up to the drummer (if you can't hear everyone else, then you're playing too loud!). Listening to Baby Dodds performing with Sidney Bechet on a live recording of "China Boy" some years ago taught me what was possible with drum dynamics. You could build up from a whisper to a freight train in a few short measures. Rehearsing with Giora Feidman in his home for the recording of "Dance of Fire," I learned what a real pianissimo (Italian for "extremely soft") on the drum set was. My actual hearing has never been 100 percent, even before playing a lot of rock and roll, but thankfully I still have enough to be able to play without amplification.

Just imagine what it must have been like for a ten-piece klezmer band in the 1920s trying to record in one room with one microphone (drums in the back indeed). I practice by listening over and over to the songs I'm learning; I record rehearsals and listen back to those recordings as well. I keep my hands in shape by warming up with brushes instead of sticks (I've also been a painter since high school, which has strengthened the muscles in my hands and wrists). I still listen to the old 78 recordings (on CDs) with headphones for the ultimate klezmer inspiration and still adhere to the adage, "one foot in tradition and one foot to the future."

When the Klezmatics first began playing music together, we all brought our own musical history with us. All of our previous musical lives converged, which led to quite a diversity. Most of us had not played klezmer music for very long. Learning the traditional sound first then using that knowledge as a jumping-off point was a very exciting process. Somehow that band has been able to stay fresh and stay together for twenty-five years now.

My first drum teacher was Sammy Anflick who had just moved to Greensboro, North Carolina (from Philadelphia), soon after I did with my family from Detroit in 1965. He taught me all the basic rudiments and gave me a jazz (improvising) sensibility early on. He designed a set of rubber practice pads that allowed me to play along to records without driving everyone out of the house. During a drum break or solo, he taught me to keep the melody of the song in my head the whole time. Sammy had played a lot of *bar mitsve* parties I went to growing up, and as it turned out he played with Mickey Katz on his "Wild West" show when it came to Philadelphia. Katz made a number of recordings that parodied Americana in a Yiddish/klezmer style, backed by top studio musicians in Los Angeles. Sammy's regular gig in Philadelphia was with singer Catarina Valente.

The first drummer to help me connect the dots from the drummers who played on the 78-rpm recordings was Sy Salzberg, who is still an active player. Sy played a lot on Broadway, and when I was working at Noise New York studio in 1985 (having just moved to New York City), he came into the recording studio with Klezmer Plus, which featured Pete Sokolow on organ, Sid Beckerman on clarinet, Howie Leess on tenor sax, and Henry Sapoznik on banjo (blessed memories Sid and Howie). I took the opportunity to focus on Sy's playing, which was really informative. I heard a flow around the drums and cymbals that was missing in my own drumming, especially the style of drumming for dancing. This flow involves fill and drum patterns that connect the measures, encouraging conversations with the rest of the band. I was fortunate to occasionally sub for Sy when Klezmer Plus got called to play some concerts out of town. Then Pete had the wonderful idea to call Irving Gratz, Dave Tarras's old drummer, to come play on the show when the band went to New York. Irving had basically retired at age eighty-six, but thankfully he agreed to join us! We did three concerts together for the Brooklyn Arts Council. It's hard to describe what it was like to watch and listen to Irving play after hearing his old recordings. The way I approached the *bulgar* beat on the snare drum was a mirror image of his approach. His left hand played straight eighth notes while his right played the accents that shaped the rhythm. My right hand played steady eighths while my left played the accents. He knew how to lift or push the band, yet his fills were different from Sy's. Irving played the final three shows in front of about three thousand people and passed away the following week, leaving quite a legacy. The Tarras Trio records are among my most coveted, and actually having met Irving Gratz makes them even more special.

At KlezKamp in Parksville, New York (the original location when this Yiddish Folk Arts retreat began), I had the opportunity to play with several master klezmer musicians, including percussionists. The two I remember fondly were Ben Bazyler and the one and only Max Epstein. The following is an interview my friend and colleague Yale Strom did with Manya Bazyler Weber about her father Ben:

My father Ben Bazyler was born in Warsaw in 1922. He learned to sing Yiddish songs and play the drums when he was eleven years old. There was always singing in his home where he learned much of his Yiddish repertoire and was self-taught on the drums. As a youth he loved to go to celebrations and enjoyed helping to create a joyous atmosphere. But he never felt he was one of the employees; he always felt he was one of the guests wherever he was hired to play the drums. My father performed on a regular trap set but also had a small drum he wore from his neck that allowed him to walk, march and bring it to a casual party without having to deal with the large trap set. He called this small drum his *baraban*. When Germany attacked Poland on September 1, 1939 my father escaped from Warsaw to the Soviet Union and quickly was put into a gulag somewhere in Siberia. Music literally saved his life; the camp guards gave him larger food rations in exchange for his entertaining them. My father was in this gulag from 1939–1946. Then when he was released he settled in Tashkent, Uzbekistan where I was born. There my father played music for the Jewish and non-Jewish communities at their parties, events and weddings. Then in 1958 my father returned to Poland moving to Lodz. He was happy to return because of his Polish heritage and loved Polish music. In Lodz he drove a taxi and performed with many different musicians Jewish and Polish music. I remember going out in the evenings with my parents to some friend's home and there would be several couples. My parents enjoyed good conversation, eating, drinking, and singing. Whether my father had his baraban or just a table top he loved to keep rhythm to whatever he was singing. Sometimes my father would give us the drum sticks and we would play on his baraban. The drum was an extension of my father and his love for music and how it brought people together. I remember songs such as "Tumbalalaika"and "My Yiddishe Mama" being sung at such gatherings. Though some people thought the word *klezmer* was a derogatory word for a Jewish musician my father never felt this way. We weren't particularly religious but I did attend a Yiddish school in the afternoons after my regular public school, we went to the synagogue on the High Holidays and we enjoyed going to the Yiddish theatre when it came to Lodz. Then in 1964 HIAS (Hebrew Immigrant Aid Society) brought my family to Minneapolis where he worked in a furniture factory and played music until we finally moved to Los Angeles in 1965. In Los Angeles my father got his barber's license and continued playing music. My father told me how many klezmer musicians in Poland also were barbers so he was kind of following this tradition in America. He joined the musicians union because he wanted to meet younger musicians, get more work, and have job security. He was always interested in learning new music. One of his favorite groups he loved to hear sing was the "Rat Pack" [Y.S.: Frank Sinatra, Dean Martin, Sammy Davis Jr., Peter Lawford, and Joey Bishop]. One group he performed with for thirty years was Stella by Starlight. They performed at all kinds of Jewish functions. They consisted of Stella the singer, my father and an accordion player. So during the 1970s and '80s you could hear my father play the drums with Stella by Starlight and singing and whistling while he cut hair at his barbershop on Fairfax Ave. When the revival of klezmer began my father always said: "There was nothing that needed to be revived; I have been playing Jewish music my whole life." He enjoyed playing for and learning from the younger klezmer musicians. He went to Klez-Kamp several times and that is where he met Dave Licht. He wanted to be included as a teacher, student, and musician. My father felt it was important to share with the next generation what he learned when he was a kid in Poland and to inspire them to continue playing klezmer.[1]

With Max Epstein we played in a trio with Pete Sokolow. Sokolow was on piano, Epstein on clarinet, and myself on drums at the legendary Paramount Hotel. Max was the oldest of four brothers, all musicians. Pete was considered the honorary "fifth" Epstein brother, who incidentally had also played keyboard for Dave Tarras. There is an amazing documentary film called *A Tickle in the Heart* that must be seen—basically a biography of the Epstein brothers. The film covers their story from Brooklyn to Berlin to Moscow and then Florida. Julie, the drummer and the youngest, is not quite retired and still plays some gigs in South Florida. Watching and listening to Julie play at the Ashkenaz Festival in Toronto some years ago made me feel like a beginner again. Big, barrel-chested Julie rolling around the drums, choking cymbals show-drummer style, had me on the edge of my seat. "Dukes of Freilachland" is a great recording of the Epsteins and a wonderful example of Julie's drumming.

Julie Epstein was more of a show drummer while Irving Gratz was a more traditional "meat and potatoes" straight-ahead drummer. Julie played a more modern drum kit with generally two tom-toms, the bass drum, and two or three cymbals to choose from. Most of Irving's drumming was about snare drum and bass drum. His woodblock patterns and cymbal crashes stand out, since most of his playing is done with the kick drum and snare. The basic difference in the way we hear Epstein and Gratz is due to the recording technology that was available during the 1920s through the '60s. I think the low-fi sound of the 78s actually has more of a punch, especially with the larger band recordings. There is a bit of mystery there that requires an acute listener. The 1950s and 1960s Epstein Brothers recordings sound like what it feels like to be at a classic Jewish wedding.

My drum set playing took a left turn when I began studying West African *djembe* drumming shortly after moving to New York City. I had played conga drums and actually made a percussion record with my brother Dennis (of blessed memory) while still living in North Carolina. We played together in the bossa nova band Minas, and the bandleader recommended I call a friend of his who was teaching in New York. I ended up marching in the Greenwich Village Halloween parade playing agogo bells in the *batucada* (carnival) band. On the way to class one night, I stumbled upon an African drumming and dance class in the same building and ended up staying. The djembe has a range of sounds unlike any drum I had heard up to that point, and I studied for almost two years, three times a week. I wrote a piece for *Modern Drummer* magazine's thirtieth anniversary book describing how the experience of learning djembe changed my concept of the drum set. It created a new "center" for me and gave me a fresh approach to the sound of drums and cymbals. I began to appreciate even more the power of the snare drum, cymbal, and woodblock on the 78-rpm klezmer recordings. It was sonically amazing how much sound could come from one instrument. Deconstructing the drum kit made me consider its origin. Photos of the old klezmer musicians showed an older man at the bass drum, another playing a pair of cymbals, and a young boy playing the snare drum. But in more modern society one drummer is able to play the role of three.

Other noted klezmer drummers and percussionists were Joe Helfenbein, who played for Joseph Cherniavsky's (1894–1959) Yiddishe American Jazz Band (with Naftule Brandwein on clarinet) that recorded a lot in the 1920s. Then there was Jacob "Jakie" Hoffman (1899–1974), who played in Harry Kandel's (1885–1943) Orchestra and only recorded with him in the 1920s and '30s. Hoffman helped to create the Philadelphia klezmer sound by playing the xylophone instead of the *tsimbl*. A xylophone virtuoso, Hoffman played with several symphony orchestras including the Philadelphia Orchestra under the baton of Eugene Ormandy and the Boston Pops under the baton of Arthur Fiedler. Finally there was Jack Saunders who played in Sam Musiker's Orchestra that recorded several klezmer albums in the 1950s.

The invention of the bass drum pedal in 1887 was the very beginning of the multi-instrumentalist drummer's being able to use hands and feet. The first pedals were difficult to operate, and not until 1909 did William F. Ludwig invent a smoother device that also included a brass rod that would simultaneously strike a small cymbal mounted nearby (boom-ting or boom-crash at the same time). Later came the sock cymbal, or low boy, a foot pedal that pushed two cymbals together. As the hardware became more sophisticated, a taller stand was invented (c. 1928), and it became known as the hi-hat, which could be played with sticks. Because of the tight space in the orchestra pit, an army of "traps" (slang for "contraption") surrounded the bass drum. There was the snare in front, tom-toms on the side and floor, mounted cymbal tree on top, as well as a woodblock and cowbell. One drummer had become an entire percussion section!

Figure 6.1 Basic klezmer rhythms.

Figure 6.2   An example of the Terkishe rhythm expressed as 12/8.

KALARASHER BULGAR

Figure 6.3 "Kalarasher Bulgar," played first as a khusidl then as a bulgar/freylekhs.

BAYM REBIN'S SUDE (Khusidl)

Figure 6.4 "Baym Rebin's Sude," a classic traditional khusidl.

A student of the drum should practice all the basic rudiments, especially the single-stroke and double-stroke rolls, paradiddles, and triplets. Play along with the recordings on a practice pad and accent along with the melodies. Here is a list of some of the most influential klezmer drummers:

Irving Gratz. He played on most of Dave Tarras's recordings in the 1920s–'40s as well as Tarras's last recording in 1979. Gratz also played with Naftule Brandwein. He was the "Sonny Greer" (Duke Ellington's classic drummer) of klezmer percussion.

Joe Helfenbein. He played with Joseph Cherniavsky's Yiddishe American Jazz Band. Once at a Jewish wedding while playing with Tarras, Helfenbein suggested to him that Tarras play at a charity banquet put on by the Progressive Musicians Benevolent Society. It was there Tarras met Joseph Cherniavsky who happened to need a new clarinetist. The clarinetist he had was Brandwein. Cherniavsky complained he was an exhibitionist with a drinking problem. So, Cherniavsky hired Tarras to replace Brandwein, which perhaps sparked an ego duel between the two virtuosi and fueled the rumor mill among klezmer musicians even today of "who was better."

Julie Epstein. He played with his brothers in their band called the Epstein Brothers. Their opus recording was "Dukes of Freilachland" where you hear Julie Epstein play. He is also featured in the documentary film about the band called *A Tickle in the Heart* (1992).

Sy Salzberg. He was a wonderful Broadway show drummer (*Man of La Mancha*) and is on many important recordings like: *The Essential Cole Porter, George Feyer Plays Gershwin*, and others. In the klezmer world, Salzberg recorded with the great klezmer clarinetist Marty Levitt on Levitt's recording *The "Undisputed" King of the Klezmers*, and he is featured on several Klezmer Plus recordings. Salzberg is an important link to the old style of klezmer drumming. He is still active, living, and playing in the metropolitan area of New York City.

Ben Bazyler. He was a klezmer drummer born in Warsaw, Poland, who eventually settled in Los Angeles. A virtuoso, Bazyler was featured on the first recording of *Brave Old World*. He also appeared at KlezKamp in the original location at the Parmount Hotel, thanks to Michael Alpert who knew him from living in Los Angeles. He was known for marching around the camp playing the poyk. Bazyler had the straightest back posture I've ever seen of a drummer sitting at his drum set, even when he was well into his seventies.

Elaine Hoffman-Watts. She is the daughter and niece of Jacob and Johnny Hoffman, respectively, who both played in Harry Kandel's Orchestra (they both played in the Philadelphia Orchestra as well). Elaine has proudly continued the family tradition of being great percussionists and is still active on the scene, playing and teaching. I have enjoyed playing many times with her over the years at KlezKamp. I was honored to be included in her own recording, *I Remember Klezmer* (from 2003). Also featured on the recording is Gerry Brown, one of her early students who has been Stevie Wonder's drummer for over twenty years.

Samuel E. "Sammy" Anflick. He was a famous jazz drummer also from Philadelphia. The founder and leader of the Klezmer Conservatory Band, Hankus Netsky, whose family is part of the Philadelphia klezmer legacy, showed me a photo of his uncle Kol Katz's Orchestra that played Jewish weddings; the drummer was Anflick. He was my first drum teacher and set me on a great path through listening to jazz and practicing the rudiments, and showed me how to strengthen my wrists. He owned a jazz club/Jewish deli in the 1970s in Greensboro, North Carolina, where I was a busboy. At this deli I heard a lot of great music and occasionally got to sit in on drums with the ensemble. Though Anflick is better known as a jazz drummer, he also performed with Mickey Katz when his "Wild West" show toured Philadelphia.

Finally, listening carefully to the rhythm of Brandwein's clarinet playing on *King of the Klezmer Clarinet* and how he seamlessly varies the melody in any one specific tune is worthy of a drummer's interpretation. Students of the drum should practice playing that melody by following the rhythm of the clarinet as closely as possible with accents on the drum pad. Take a section at a time and play each figure slowly. I find playing along with tracks that have no drums even more challenging than emulating each drum, cymbal, and woodblock on the tracks listed below. Immerse yourself in the sound by closing your eyes and trying to visualize yourself in the recording studio with these master klezmer musicians.

The *King of the Klezmer Clarinet* features the great clarinetist Naftule Brandwein. The songs on this CD were superbly restored by the sound technician Jack Towers. For maximum fidelity I still recommend closed-ear headphones. This compilation of different Brandwein recordings gives the student who is studying the drum a wide variety of styles that supported the gutsy full sound of the clarinet. The contrast between the 1923–1926 and 1941 sessions is dramatic, not only the clarinet playing but the drumming as well. To my ears, despite the improved technology and sonically cleaner sound, the drumming sounds a bit choppy on the 1941 session. You can hear a crisper snare drum and woodblock, and the cymbal requires less of a "squint" to hear the rhythm. However the 1920s sessions have more character, more personality. Perhaps because they used fewer microphones there is a smoother sonic blend. The snare drums have more punch, the cymbals are not as sharp, and I prefer the different woodblock sounds. Most likely different woodblocks were used at each session. Mookie Brandwein connects with brother Naftule and nothing sounds forced.

When I spoke with the klezmer pianist Pete Sokolow and klezmer clarinetist Joel Rubin, they both agreed the drummer on the 1923–1926 sessions was Naftule's brother Mookie. Rubin told me that the 1941 session was played by Max Goldberg. Rubin heard this from Goldberg himself. However Sokolow, never shy to give his opinion, told in no uncertain terms this was not Goldberg. In fact, he said it could have been any one of these Jewish drummers who was gigging in and around New York City at the time. Sokolow mentioned: Whitey Stilowitzky, Murray Kalevsky, Hal Bennis, Charlie and Willie Corman, and European-born Israel (Irving) Torgman. Irving Gratz and Julie Epstein took lessons from Torgman, wanting to pick up on his particular playing style. Gratz also played with both Brandwein ("who just let me play") and Tarras ("who tried to control me"). However, the more I listened to these Brandwein tracks, the more I hear someone other than Gratz because of the different woodblock patterns and how he hits the crash cymbal. On this recording I recommend listening to all the tracks. The standouts that have an incredible rhythmic feel are No. 13, "Fun Tashlach" and No. 19, "Turkishe Yalle Vey Uve Tanz" (Brandwein's variation of the melody is pure genius). Then there is track No. 21, "Araber Tanz" (this is a terkisher that segues to a bulgar); No. 22, "Nifty's Eigene" (the woodblock pattern sounds like Elaine Hoffman-Watts); and No. 23, "Fufzehn Yahr Fon Der Heim Awek" (there is a wonderful call-and-response segment between the clarinet and trombone that sounds like Yiddish blues).

DISCOGRAPHY

The Klezmatics, *Rhythm and Jews* (Rounder Records, 2003). Listen to all the tracks.
The Klezmatics, *Rise Up—Shtety Oyf!* (Rounder Records, 2003). Listen to all the tracks.
Sapoznik, Henry, and Spottswood, Dick, *Klezmer Pioneers* (Rounder Records, 1993). Listen specifically to track 15, "A Labediga Honga." This is a medium-fast bulgar with cymbal and woodblock.
Schwartz, Martin, *Klezmer Music 1908–1927* (Martin Schwartz Folk collection, 2009). Listen specifically to track 14, "Turkish Yelle Vey Uve," for the rhythm of the clarinet, and to track 17, "Oy Tate, Sis Gut," for the rhythm of the snare and woodblock.
Strom, Yale, *Borsht with Bread, Brothers* (ARC, 2007). Listen specifically to the improvisation I am doing with Hot Pstromi on track 10, "Kalarasher Bulgar," and to track 12, "Ben Avrameni."
Tarras, Dave, *Yiddish-American Klezmer Music 1925–1956* (Shanachie, 1992). Listen particularly to the snare drum and how it alternates with the woodblock on track 16, "Branas Hassene," and to the rhythm of the *doina*, turkisher, bulgar, and freilach on track 23.

NOTE

1. Interview with Manya Bazyler Weber (originally from Tashkent, Uzbekistan) on the telephone in her home in Los Angeles with Yale Strom, April 26, 2012.

7

Violin

Yale Strom

The violinist was to the klezmer band what the cantor was to his parishioners—the vessel from which all manner of human emotions flowed. The ebb and flow of emotion that a cantor elicits from a prayer with his melisma voicings, which in turn move the parishioners to sing to God in heaven with such ecstasy (in Yiddish, *dveykes*), is the same primary function of the lead violinist in a klezmer band. The klezmer violinist prays rather than plays on his instrument.

From the mid-sixteenth century (when the violin as we know it today was invented) through the beginning of the twentieth century, the violinist served as lead figure for and symbol of klezmer music. During my ethnographic treks to Central and Eastern Europe, I saw violins etched as decorative art images into the Torah arks at several synagogues (such as in Poland), carved into Jewish tombstones in Dorohoi, Romania; Soroca, Moldova; and Prague, Czech Republic (where one of the earliest klezmer guilds began in 1558 with the violin as their symbol), and painted on the ceiling of a synagogue alongside zodiac motifs in Vaslui, Romania. There could be no more literal illustration of the violin's reputation within the Jewish community as a distinctively "Jewish instrument."

Before the nineteenth century and the introduction of woodwinds and brass, most klezmer bands consisted of strings (violin, cello, bass, *tsimbl*/hammer dulcimer), percussion (Turkish drum, cymbals, bass drum, woodblock), and some plectrum instruments (mandolin, *bandura*[1] in southwestern Ukraine, and *cobza*[2] in Bessarabia). Although the clarinet began to grow in popularity in the last decades of the nineteenth century, the violin remained the favorite of Jewish klezmer players, in large part because of how the violin's sonority was closely identified with the human voice. In Tomashov (Tomaszow Lubelski), Poland, community members said as much:

When the wedding guests had gathered around the *rebe* [Yiddish for "Khasidic leader"], in walked Shulik, who immediately stretched his right hand out to the rebe while the left one held the violin. The rebe shook Shulik's hand and said, "Sing to our God with the violin." With his beating oblong fingers, which so deftly and tremulously dashed back and forth upon the fiddle, Shulik proceeded from the depths of his soul to touch upon the precious strings of his heart. His music caused a river of tears to flow from the women, who sat still and quiet in the room. Shulik's fiddle was able to take you from the greatest feeling of sadness one moment and throw you into a joyous mood the next moment. In such an ecstatic atmosphere one could not help but allow one's feet to dance.[3]

In this respect, the klezmer violinist operated as an extension of the cantor's voice. "The cantor made a *krekht* [Yiddish for "groan, moan"] from the neck up and a klezmer made a krekht from the neck down."[4] His ability to imitate the crying, ululating, moaning, and laughing cantorial techniques he had heard since he was an infant in the synagogue was shaped into specific klezmer ornamentations. The klezmer's conservatory was the synagogue, his lessons the daily prayers, and his concerts the Jewish holidays. According to the cantor Abraham-Moshe Bernshteyn (born in Vilna, 1866–1932), the krekht was the cornerstone of Jewish music: "It was an outbreak of ecstatic joy. It was the source of exaltation and spirited pleasure for the masses of Eastern European Jews."[5]

A number of well-known klezmer violinists either started their musical careers as cantors or they had a family member (father, grandfather, uncle) who was a noted cantor. We have firsthand information about some of these klezmer violinists from Joachim Stutschewsky (a cellist)[6] who himself came from an illustrious klezmer family and who later became a famous musicologist in Israel. What is important about Stutschewsky's research is that it shines a light on the klezmer musicians of Western Galicia (Tarnopol, Lemberg—Lviv, Premishlan—Przemyslany, Rzeszow, etc.) especially the violinists, while most of what we know from other written sources about the klezmer violinist are about those from Eastern Ukraine and Bessarabia. In his book *Ha-Klezmorim* (Hebrew for "The Klezmers"), Stutschewsky writes about the Weintraub family of Brod (Brody) and the Wolfstahls of Tarnopol, both of which produced great cantors and klezmer violinists. Here is an account of the strong competition between two other known klezmer ensembles in Brod in the mid-nineteenth century:

> Besides Tshortkever's Yosi-V'ovi (Weintraub) klezmer band there were two other famous bands in Brod. One was called the Blacks (the Topaz family) and the other The Reds (the Rosenblum family). The Topaz family got their name from their dark beards and mustaches and the Rosenblum's got theirs from having red and yellow beards. They hated each other and fought among themselves all the time. The Reds were more successful securing work in the city theatre and accompanying the famous Brody Singers.[7] This created even more jealousy between the two bands. There were daily fist fights between members of each band in the town despite people trying to make peace between the two daily. This fighting continued until the chief of police was to marry the wealthy Count Rusotski's daughter. Of course such an important and lucrative wedding created even more hostility between the Reds and the Blacks until Kalir the Jewish pharmacist and bonesetter, and one of the elders of the community decided to put a stop to this fighting. He and the elders felt this fighting made the Jews look bad in front of their gentile neighbors. He put his foot down and created a band made up of musicians from both warring

ensembles. At the wedding a miracle happened. During one of the fast dance numbers the klezmer musicians from both bands realized that each musician was a great musician and even better person. After this wedding there was never any fighting between these two ensembles. Because of the peace the local government gave Kalir an honorary position as head of the city council.[8]

Another valuable resource for learning more about the klezmer violinist and the life of a klezmer in Galicia during the interwar period is Leopold Kozlowski. I met Leopold Kozlowski in 1981 at his home in Krakow while on my first ethnographic trek through Central and Eastern Europe looking for remnants of klezmer history and music. Leopold's grandfather was Peysekh Brandwein (Peysekh ben Tsvi) who was born in Premishlan (Przemyslany, Ukraine) around 1835 and died in 1919. The Brandwein family were followers of and close friends with the Premishlaner *rebe* Rabbi Meir ben Aaron Leyb (1780–1850) and the subsequent Presmishlaner rebes through the eve of World War II. Peysekh had fourteen children (Elia, Feige-Bleema, Moshe, Azriel, Henrietta and Naftulah [twins], Mendl, Arumcha, Leiza, Zilpah, Tzudik, Mordechai, Yankel, Hersch) with four different wives (maiden names of three: Herman, Hirsch, Kleinman). Of the fourteen, nine were boys, all of whom played at some time in Peysekh's klezmer ensemble that was known throughout Galicia. Typical of most Galicianer klezmer ensembles, the leader (in Yiddish, *kapel-mayster*) played the violin.

> My grandfather's klezmer band was known throughout Galicia, which then was part of the Austro-Hungarian Empire. They performed at Jewish and gentile weddings especially those of the rich, all the fancy balls, for Count Petoski, they even played several times for King Franz Joseph. The king considered my grandfather's klezmer band as his own Jewish klezmer musicians.[9]

Brandwein's ensemble was typical of many of the large klezmer ensembles prior to World War I, in that it was made up of mostly strings (led by the first violinist), a clarinet, trumpet, tsimbl, and accordion. What was not typical was the inclusion of an accordionist in the band. Peysekh Brandwein was known as a virtuoso violinist and composer. The repertoire of his ensemble was primarily his own compositions.

> Once at a wedding the bride requested a certain wedding march from my grandfather while the bride was accompanied to the wedding canopy. It was like when Kol Nidre was recited on Yom Kiper eve—everyone knew this wedding march and everyone knew it was composed by Peysekh Brandwein. This tune was performed by many other klezmer bands throughout Galicia.[10]

Within Galicia every klezmer band had its own specific territory in which they could ply their trade. This meant that they could perform legally there without getting into trouble from another band. The consequences of not playing within your boundaries could be a fine levied by the Jewish community against the musicians, a rebuke from the local rabbi or *Khasidic* rebe that carried an embarrassing stigma, or being embroiled in a fistfight. The legal right to perform in a specific region was called *khazoke* (Yiddish for "the claim to, the right, the tenure"). It prevented other klezmer bands from "setting up shop" in just any town and guaranteed the hereditary rights of the klezmer families within each ensemble.

My grandfather had the khazoke to play in Premishlan and surrounding villages like Svirzh, Polochov [Poluchiv], Hanaczow [Hanachiv], and Borshchiv [Borshchov]. However in towns and cities like Bibrka, Rohaytn, Lemberg, [Lviv] Tarnopol, Drohobych, and Stanislaw [Ivano Frankisv'k], my grandfather had to share the region with the klezmers from Gline [Hlynyany] who belonged to Moshe Mikhl Dudlzack. There was some friendly competition between the Brandwein's and Dudlzacks, in fact there was a drummer/dancer from the Dudlzack family, Aron Leybl Dudlzack that was a member of my grandfather's band. However my grandfather was such a great violinist people requested him for their weddings even in Gline [Y.S.: 25 kilometers to the north of Premishlan], so sometimes he'd just take two other musicians with him from his band and play for the *baveynen* [Yiddish for "the crying of the bride"], the wedding ceremony and a few special tunes for the in-laws at the wedding party. However the Gline klezmer band was not allowed to play in Premishlan while the Brandweins still lived and performed there. After my grandfather died all the sons except two immigrated to America. Only Elia the oldest and my father the youngest stayed behind. The only two who kept playing klezmer music as their main livelihood in America were Azriel and Naftule. Both did well but Naftule really became famous for his particular clarinet style which was more influenced by the Gypsies [Y.S.: Roma] that came from Constantinople. My father's klezmer band consisted of four violins, two first and two second, cello, three clarinets, A-flat, E-flat and C, two flautists, two *tsimbalists*, contrabass and drum. It was not a big drum but a Jewish drum that you held by a strap that was wrapped around your waist that had a small cymbal on top. When the Depression came it hurt all the klezmer musicians throughout the Galicia. In 1931 Moshe Mikhl Dudlzack immigrated to Argentina. He captured a bit more work because the Gline klezmer ensemble under the leadership of violinist Yermye [Jerimiah][11] Hescheles was not nearly as good as Dudlzack ensemble and my father was a much better violinist than Hescheles. My father studied classical violin at the Lemberg [L'viv, Ukraine] conservatory. But work was becoming scarcer and anti-Semitism was growing so when my father received an invitation in 1933 from Dudlzack to come to Argentina because there was plenty of work he left immediately. My father formed a klezmer ensemble and was the conductor of the symphony orchestra in Tres Arroyos. He returned in 1937 to Premishlan and formed another klezmer band that I played in until the war began in 1941. The band consisted of my father playing first violin, my brother Dulko playing second and sometimes doubling the first violin part, Shiye Tsimbler who was from the Dudlzack family, a brilliant tsimbalist, Hirshele Dudlzack son of Aron Leybl played drums, Dugi Brandwein second violin and me on accordion or sometimes piano. Those years just before the war it was economically so hard my father played for anyone anywhere and taught music as well. We played not only weddings but for the Yiddish theatre, silent movies, cabarets, balls, dance classes even for Baptisms. Tragically my father along with three hundred sixty other Jewish men from Premishlan were shot on November 5, 1941 and buried in the Hanachov [Hanachivka, Ukraine] forests.[12]

At this same time in America the recording industry (Victor, Columbia, Decca, Emerson) realized they could sell "nostalgia" to the immigrant population, and this was a large, seemingly endless market to be exploited, so ethnic records of various genres began to be recorded including klezmer and Yiddish songs. In the early recordings the melody was driven by unison lines from such instruments as the trumpet, clarinet, and violin. These early recordings standardized klezmer tunes that had been for years played in different versions depending on the klezmer and where he lived. These early recordings created a kind of "codification" for what these klezmer tunes should sound like. Thus other musicians copied the sound they heard from the recordings because it was considered the correct and "original" way these tunes had been performed in Eastern Europe. Then Abe Schwartz, a Romanian violinist and pianist, came up with the idea that a single instrument could be the lead on the melody and even improvise a solo as well. This was probably an idea that he derived from hearing early jazz greats like Louis Armstrong, Sydney Bechet, and King Oliver. Consequently clarinet soloists like Dave Tarras, Naftule Brandwein, Shloimke Beckerman, and eventually Max Epstein began to push aside the klezmer violinists as the "go to" instrumentalists in these early ethnic recordings, because clarinet was popular in America through the jazz recordings, and it could be heard above the din of a band when everyone was playing tutti. The violin could not compete with the clarinet in terms of volume and especially over the din of the drummer.

Another reason for the demise of the violin as the lead instrument in a klezmer band was that the quality of the klezmer clarinetists was higher than the violinists. This opinion is based upon the klezmer recordings we have from the 1920s and '30s. There were good klezmer violinists like Abe Schwartz and Berish Katz, but they were overshadowed by the virtuosity and personalities of Brandwein, Beckerman, and Tarras. These three clarinetists in particular became famous among the Jews and some non-Jews because they were heard weekly on popular Yiddish radio programs, in the Yiddish theater, on recordings, and in the Catskills during the summer.

Finally with the Depression, less klezmer music was being recorded. Most immigrants were interested in becoming assimilated into the new world, not preserving the culture of the old. Consequently klezmer musicians found themselves crossing into other musical genres. For the klezmer violinists this would be the difficult (often snobbish) world of classical music, and for the wind players they had the choice of playing classical and/or popular music, which was jazz at the time. Consequently there were some great klezmer musicians like the Muziker brothers, Sam (tenor sax) and Ray (clarinet), who played in both genres (klezmer and jazz) and others like Ziggy Elman (trumpet) and Manny Klein, who started off in klezmer but really made their mark in jazz.

By the turn of the twentieth century, massive Jewish emigration and the number of Jews killed during World War I had caused the decline of klezmer musicians in Eastern Europe, but still many plied their trade. It was the only thing they knew to make a living. The heyday for the klezmer violinist had been during the nineteenth century through the eve of World War I. However the tradition of the klezmer violinist who

represented the personality and artistry of his band through his leadership and virtuosic playing still existed in parts of Poland, Romania, and the Soviet Union through
the eve of the Holocaust.

Of the many great klezmer violinists throughout the nineteenth and the beginning
of the twentieth centuries, only a few reached such renown that legends were created
around them. To have any one of these violinists at a wedding or some other affair
said to the Jewish community that this was not an ordinary celebration.

In the first half of the nineteenth century, Shmuel Tshortkev (family name,
Weintraub) and his son Yosi-V'ovi became the nucleus of the Tshortkever klezmer
ensemble in Brod (Brody). Shmuel played mainly his own compositions, and one in
particular was called "The Deer Hunter," based on the lament of David for Jonathan
(I Samuel 19). According to Stutschewsky, the father and son created a whole musical
fantasy and would play this written piece for nearly an hour without any improvisation in the synagogue just after the Sabbath ended.

> Shmuel and his son immersed themselves in it and expressed the happiness and sorrow of
> Israel, the terror of exile, the mercy of God, the love of the Torah, the longing to return
> and the depths of prayer and entreaties of the soul.[13]

After Shmuel's death Yosi-V'ovi led the klezmer ensemble to even greater fame in
Brod. His name carried such weight that all the wealthy Jewish families and many
wealthy gentile families never planned a wedding without first securing the date from
Yosi-V'ovi.

Avram-Moyshe Kholdenok, better known by his nickname Pedutser (1928–1902),
was born in Radomsyl (Radomisl, Ukraine), near Kiev. (His name means "the rock re-
deemed" in Hebrew. Gamliel ben Pedutser [Pedahzur in the Torah] was a member of
the Tribe of Menasseh and was one of those chosen by Moses to bring an offering for
the new Tabernacle: Numbers 1:10, 23.) Pedutser grew up in a family that followed
the teachings of the Kartshever Khasidim. When he left home he settled in Berdichev,
Ukraine, where he gained a reputation as the "lord" of the klezmers. At a wedding,
after the band had played a few tunes and had warmed up the guests, Pedutser would
come out holding his violin and walking like a king, surrounded by complete silence.
He was also famous among the wealthy Russians and Ukrainians. "When I play for
the poor I am the most important dish, and when I play for the rich my violin sounds
like jewelry, but all they want to do is eat."[14]

Pedutser loved to show off his talents, imitating birdcalls on his violin or juggling
the violin and bow. But he was foremost an artist. His band with thirteen musicians
was famous throughout Berdichev and its environs. To play with Pedutser was a
great honor. Natan Sapir played violin and was the leader of the band when Pedutser
was not there. In and around Berdichev, his music was the "meat and potatoes" of
most of the klezmer bands for fifty years. Unfortunately only a few of his tunes have
survived.

A competitor of Pedutser's was Alter Tchudnover (1846–1912), who was born
in Tchudnow, Poland (Cudniv, Ukraine). Instead of birdcalls, Tchudnover became

famous for the train sounds and whistles he made on his violin. One of the most famous klezmers in Eastern Europe, he wrote music that made people laugh and cry. He owned two violins—one a cheap one he played with his band, the other his Amati,[15] which he played as a soloist. One wealthy Russian merchant was so impressed by Tchudnover's Amati that he offered to buy it. At first Tchudnover refused, but eventually he gave in, and in exchange the Russian merchant built him a huge home with a large stone wall surrounding it.

Tchudnover's talent carried over to his nephew, student and band member Louis Grupp (1888–1983), who immigrated to America.

> Sure we read music; he taught us. We practiced Kreutzer, Screidek [popular music method books of the day]. My uncle used to get sheet music like this with a melody and he used to orchestrate it. He had a brother in America who used to send him big music, overture selections. My cousin that went to the Conservatory in Warsaw used to send me his book.[16]

Then there was Yosle Druker (1822–1879) known to everyone only by his nickname: Stempenyu. He was immortalized by the great Yiddish writer Sholem Aleichem (1859–1916) in his novella *Stempenyu*. The book, written in 1888, was the first Sholem Aleichem story translated into other languages, first German in 1889 and then English in 1913. It made Stempenyu's legacy greater that it already was. Stempenyu was born with klezmer in his blood: he came from ten generations of klezmer musicians. His father Beryl Bass played the bass, his grandfather Shmulik Trompeyt played the trumpet, his great-grandfather Feyvish played the tsimbl, and his great-great-grandfather Efrayim played the flute. Beryl did not read music, but his son was sent to a private teacher. At fifteen, Stempenyu left his father's house and toured the country as a kind of freelance klezmer, joining whatever klezmer band needed a violinist. By eighteen he had his own ensemble in Odessa and was known for his virtuosity as well as his composing skills. Eventually he settled down in Berdichev and continued to polish his reputation. One listener commented:

> Every place Stempenyu went, everyone wanted to see him open his case. When he put the violin under his chin the rest of the violin players felt like burying themselves alive. He was envied by the men and eyed by the women.[17]

Sholem Aleichem wrote:

> The public sits with great respect as the klezmer plays a cheerless *moralne* [Yiddish for "moral"] (a display piece played rubato with a great deal of improvisation), a tearful one. This violin cries while the fat strings are worshipped . . . and every *krekhts* from the violin—*tiokh, tiokh, tiokh*—called out to the wedding guests and continue to echo in their hearts; in every heart, but especially in the Jewish heart. Such a violin he held. He squeezed the different strings and mostly sad and tearful songs came out . . . For such a mood one only needed the tight musicians, a skillful one, a klezmer, such a skillful one as Stempenyu was.[18]

The Berdichev tradition of producing great klezmer violinists lasted until almost the eve of World War II with Wolf Tcherniowski (1841–1930), who was Stempenyu's brother-in-law. He inherited the leadership of Stempenyu's ensemble and was a very successful klezmer even though he could not read music. He used his financial success to start a brick factory, which became one of the largest in Berdichev. His son David became the leader of the ensemble after Tcherniowski died.

Next to the great klezmer tradition of Berdichev, Bessarabia provided a rich pool of klezmer violinists including: Khayim Fiedler of Orhei and Selig Itsik Lemish (1819–1891) of Balti, (famously known as Belts)—both cities are in Moldova today. The Lemish family ensemble was very famous throughout Bessarabia and Moldavia, but their reputation went far beyond these borders. When the Italian Opera Company in the early twentieth century came to perform at the Romanian National Theatre in Bucharest they specifically asked for the Lemish klezmer ensemble to be part of the orchestra.

Some klezmer musicians chose the profession, but for most, the profession chose them. The klezmer was part of a chain leading from one generation to the next, from father to son to grandson. If a man was not born into a klezmer family and wanted to become one, it was certainly possible but more difficult. He had to learn an instrument on his own or from another klezmer. Most klezmer musicians could not pay for private lessons; consequently a father would not only teach his son about the traditions and music but how to play his own instrument. If the son could master everything the father could teach him on the violin, and even surpass his father in technique, then, in some instances, the father got him private lessons or sent him away to learn from a master teacher.

Whether a young boy learned from his father, uncle, grandfather, or was sent away to another teacher, the core techniques of klezmer music could not be learned from a methodology book (as none had been written) but only through listening, watching, and mimicking. To execute the playing of any klezmer tune or make an adopted melody (Polish, Romanian, Ruthenian, Ukrainian, etc.) more klezmerlike, the klezmer had to have the knowledge and ability to incorporate the *dreydlekh*[19] (Yiddish for "twists, turns, ornaments") into the tune. Some of these dreydlekh began to be heard less and less from the American-born klezmer violinists (beginning in the 1940s) as their classical training began to push out the more "folksy fiddler" style of playing the violin. It was only when the klezmer revival began in the mid-1970s that klezmer violinists and other instrumentalists began to listen and study the oldest 78 LPs (from before World War I) when the dreydlekh began to be heard again at Jewish celebrations.

Incorporated into any tune, but especially in display pieces like the *doyne*, moralne, *vulekhl*, or *zogekhts*, these dreydlekh gave klezmer its unique Jewish sound, especially when played on the violin. The respect the klezmer violinist who used these dreydlekh received from audiences everywhere cannot be overstated. His music was a form of therapy before music therapy ever became an academic subject, as this statement attests: "Many Jews found solace from studying the Torah, the klezmer violinist gave solace by singing the Torah."[20]

Two of the leading Jewish musicologists of the twentieth century, Arno Nadel[21] and Abraham Z. Idelsohn,[22] had their own criteria that defined the components of a Jewish melody. Nadel said there were seven criteria found in the Jewish repertoire, though not all tunes met all seven:

1. There was a recitative and melismatic quality to the melody.
2. The melody was based upon a diatonic scale.
3. The rhythm was strong and often anapestic (the first two notes accented and short, followed by a long note).
4. The melodies incorporated fifths and octaves.
5. The melody was meditative.
6. The melody mixed different voices.
7. The melody incorporated improvisation.[23]

As for Idelsohn he said, "We see that just as the Jew, being of Semitic stock, is part of the oriental world, so Jewish music—coming to life in the Near East—is, generally speaking, of one piece with the music of the Orient."[24]

In Yiddish these modes are called *shteygers* (meaning, manners, ways, kinds, modes) and form the basis of most of the klezmer repertoire. The mode can start on any note; however one must remember the intervals between the notes. The modes are comprised of more than seven notes. As I tell my students, to play a klezmer melody you need the black keys, white keys, and the gray keys. These modes should not be thought of in the Western system of twelve equal intervals to the octave. These modes are similar to those played in the indigenous folk music of the Middle East, where they use quarter tones and other microtonal intervals not found in typical Western folk music.

Each Jewish mode creates a specific mood that envelops the tune being performed. Their main musical property was the use of variant scales based on the Dorian (d e f g a b c d) and Phrygian (e f g a b c d e) tetrachordal modes. The following four modes gave klezmer music its distinct Semitic sound (similar to Turkish and Arab *maqams*), and Idelsohn identified them by the name of the Sabbath prayer that contained these modes and were sung to:

- The *Ahava Raba* (Hebrew for "a great love") is known as a *freygish* among klezmers today (d e-flat f-sharp g a b-flat c d). It is a displaced harmonic minor scale (played from the fifth step of that scale). The occasional raising of the penultimate note of the scale (d e-flat f-sharp g a b-flat c-sharp d) creates another augmented second. This scale has a distinct Arabic feel, sometimes known as the Gypsy or *Hedjaz-Kar* mode, and it is also often used by the muezzin when he calls his fellow Muslims to prayer.
- The *Mogen-Avos* (Hebrew for "guardian of our father") mode is the same as the Aeolian mode (natural minor scale). The sixth and the seventh might be raised in ascending melodic environments, as in the melodic minor scale.

- When the Ahava Raba and Mogen Avos modes were combined, the scale was known as *Mishebeyrakh* (Hebrew for "He who blesses") or sometimes *Ov-Horakhamim* (Hebrew for "father of mercy")—d e f g-sharp a b c d. It can be viewed as an altered Dorian (with a raised fourth). As with the Mogen-Avos mode, the sixth and seventh can be altered as in the melodic minor scale. Much of the southern Ukrainian and Romanian klezmer repertoire utilized this mode; it was thus sometimes referred to as the "Jewish" scale by both klezmer musicians and non-Jewish musicians.
- The *Adonoy Molekh* (Hebrew for "the Lord is king") mode is the same as the Mixolydian mode (d e f-sharp g a b c d). The seventh can be raised in ascending environments. Many Khasidic melodies from sects in Galicia (e.g., Belz, Bobov, Boyan, Dinov, Grodjisk) used this mode.

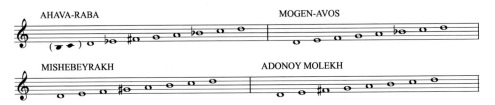

Figure 7.1   Common klezmer scales (modes).

The root of klezmer music—what made it sound "Jewish"—was not to be found in the indigenous folk music of Central or Eastern Europe but in the meditative chants and prayers of our Middle Eastern ancestors and neighbors.

By the end of the nineteenth century, many young klezmer violinists had obtained permission from the Czar to study in the music conservatories of St. Petersburg under Leopold Auer (in Hungarian: *Auer Lipót*, 1845–1930, born in Veszprem, Hungary) and Odessa under Pjotr Solomonovich Stolyarsky (1871–1944, born in Lipovtsy, Ukraine, who heard the famous Peysekh Brandwein family klezmer band play at Jewish weddings). Stolyarsky was born into a klezmer family and played several years with his family klezmer band before entering the music conservatory in Odessa, eventually becoming the head of it in 1920. The "Russian school" led by Auer grew out of the nineteenth-century Belgian Henri Vieuxtemps (1820–1881) and Belgian Eugene Ysaye (1858–1931). Auer created a unique "Russian sound" by combining some of the violin techniques the klezmer violinists had been using for years with classical techniques. Klezmer violinists used a lot of vibrato and portamento with their left hand; they also held the violin securely under the chin (unlike most folk fiddlers), using various kinds of shoulder pads. This relieved their left hand of any responsibility for holding the instrument, which allowed them to concentrate freely upon fingering, ornamentation, and vibrato. They also held the bow closer to the nut and more firmly (also uncommon among folk fiddlers), with their bow arm held freely away from the body, giving them a more natural and powerful stroke. Thus the Russian classically trained violinists became famous for their broad, sumptuous tone. Subsequently students studying classical violin today at such music conservatories as Julliard, Mannes, and Curtis do not realize that the antecedents of what they are learning in terms of how to play their violin come from the Jewish folk musicians—in other words, from the klezmers, many of whom could not read music.

Some young klezmer violinists went on to become classical musicians in orchestras, never to return to klezmer again. Others kept their feet in both the classical and klezmer worlds (affecting the klezmer's style of playing and the band's repertoire); a few became world-famous virtuosi. Some of the most famous child prodigies weaned on klezmer include:

Bronislaw Huberman (1882–1947) of Czestochowa, Poland. His first teacher was Isidor Rosen Lotto (1840–1937), who taught a six-year-old Huberman klezmer melodies Lotto learned from his father, who had been a klezmer. Seeing that Huberman was a *wunderkind*, he sent him at age seven to Berlin to one of the world's most famous violin teachers of his day, Joseph Joachim (1831–1907; he also taught Auer, among others). Eventually Huberman founded the Israeli Philharmonic Orchestra; he got the idea when he saw how many great Jewish musicians had been persecuted and forced from their jobs by the Nazis in Germany and Austria beginning in 1933.

Efrem Aleksandrovich Zimbalist (1889–1985), born in Rostov-on-Don, Russia. He heard klezmer music from his grandfather, a *tsimbalist*. His father was a conductor, and by the age of nine, Efrem Zimbalist was first violin in his father's orchestra. At age twelve he entered the St. Petersburg Conservatory and studied under Auer.

Mischa Elman or **Mikhail Saulovich** (1891–1967), born in Talnoye (Tal'ne, Ukraine). His grandfather was a klezmer violinist from Uman. It became apparent when Mischa was very young that he had perfect pitch, but his father hesitated about a career as a musician, since musicians were not very high on the social scale. He finally gave in and gave Mischa a miniature violin on which he soon learned several tunes by himself and soon after introduced Mischa to Alter Chudnower. After a short while Chudnower realized the youngster had a massive amount of talent and was able to set up an audition that eventually got him accepted to the St. Petersburg Conservatory, which was under the leadership of Leopold Auer. Mischa Elman was all of eleven when he began his classical studies.

David Fyodorovich Oistrakh (1908–1977), born in Odessa. He learned a few klezmer tunes from his father, an amateur violinist, before he began to study at age six with Stolyarsky. In June 1981, I met David Kamhi, a classical violinist and a pupil of Oistrakh's, in Sarajevo, Bosnia. Oistrakh had kept up the tradition of first teaching klezmer tunes to his pupils; he taught Kamhi a doyne because it had a lot of ornamented and repeated sixteenths—and thirty-second-note runs.

Jascha Heifetz (1901–1987), born in Vilna (Vilnius, Lithuania), and **Nathan Milstein** (1904–1992), born in Odessa. While there is no direct klezmer connection to either of them, it makes logical sense that Heifetz, who studied under Auer, and Milstein, who studied under Stolyarsky, more than likely heard and learned some klezmer.

These and other Jewish violinists became household names in many Jewish homes. As a result, by the turn of the twentieth century, the violin had become known as the Jewish instrument, so much so that if a family could afford it, violin lessons were given to all the boys in the family. "My son the violinist," were the words many Jewish parents proudly declared to their family, friends, and acquaintances—only to be transformed to "my son the doctor" two generations later.

Klezmer melodies are defined by rhythmic elements that are particular to that genre of dance (e.g., *freylekhs, hora, khusidl, onga*) and the modes on which they are based. These elements influence the style, tempo, and chords used for the accompaniment. Accompaniments can be as simple as the bass playing on the off beats or a bit more challenging, with the bass and accordion, for example, trading beats. For example, in a freylekhs (medium- to fast-tempo circle or chain dance in either 2/4 or 4/4) the rhythm can sometimes be even more rhythmically colorful, with the bass playing quarter notes while the accordion plays eighth notes. Chords used to accompany klezmer melodies reflect the modes in which a tune is based. Sometimes there is more than one chord that can be played under the melodic passage—the choice is a personal one. In traditional klezmer melodies, the chords change less often. However in modern klezmer tunes that are mixed with other genres of music like jazz, Balkan, Roma, etc., the chording can be more complex.

Though the violinist was often the leader of the klezmer ensemble and was expected to play the melody for most of the duration of a particular dance, what was equally as vital (if not sometimes more vital) than the notes was the bowing. The klezmer instilled energy into his violin through his bowing techniques. Through the use of different bow-strokes, like legato, slurs, staccato, spiccato, etc., as well as bow lengths and pressure, the violinist influenced the tenor of the tune.

Each dance melody had its own particular choreography, some of which we know today, but many dances have been lost. The dances could be as simple as a khusidl with two sections or more complicated as a *kolomeyke* with four sections. The section could be four, eight, ten, or twelve bars that usually repeated. The tunes at a traditional Jewish wedding over one hundred years ago could be played for up to fifteen minutes or until the dancers became too fatigued to continue. Today at Jewish weddings, often the hora dance set (in which tune after tune segue into each other), where the bride and groom are lifted in their chairs while others dance around them, might be only fifteen or twenty minutes in total. Tunes played at a concert go as long as the performers decide and as long as the audience is engaged.

Since the antecedents of playing klezmer on the violin come from liturgical and secular singing of Jewish music, there are many tunes that derive their Hebrew name from the daily and holiday synagogue prayers. Many of these *nigunim* (Hebrew for "melodies") come from the Khasidim, for example, "Ki One Amekho" (Hebrew for "We Are Your People") sung by the Ger Khasidim on *Rosh Hashone*; "Ate Bokhartanu" (Hebrew for "You Have Chosen Us") sung by the Koydinover Khasidim; "Hu Moshieynu" (Hebrew for "God Is Our Savior") sung by the Lubavitcher Khasidim during the weekly and Sabbath prayer services; and "Yom L'yaboshe" (Hebrew for

"From Sea to Dry Land") was recited by the Ropshitser Khasidim on the seventh day of Passover. The ornamentation of these kinds of tunes is related to the vocal styles. These melodies are sung slowly with great devotion. When there are no lyrics or the singer wants to go beyond the lyrics (and not repeat them) to a deeper more intimate connection to God, then vocalized syllables (*oy, ay, day, bim, bom, vay*) are sung to the melodies. These tunes were repeated over and over, occasionally with slight variations, sometimes up to an hour or longer. When playing Khasidic nigunim on the violin, it helps to sing along, which creates a physical and spiritual effect on the mind and body.

Invariably, klezmer tunes are repeated because they are for the most part tunes that were sung and/or danced to. The violinist (or any musician playing the melody) would vary the tune by subtly changing the melody, octaves, rhythm, note values, bowing, and ornamentations. Often in a klezmer band more than one instrument would play the melody, simultaneously resulting in melodic variants of the same tune. This sonic texturing known as heterophony was commonly heard in synagogue communal prayers. The same prayer was recited or sung to the same melody but with different tempi, vocal timbres, rhythms, and accents, which created this heterophonic sound. Subsequently, what the klezmer violinist heard and did in the confines of the synagogue, he repeated through his instrument at a Jewish wedding.

Improvisation did occur in klezmer. The lead melody instrumentalist, for example, the violinist, after having played the particular dance tune three or four times then would improvise in the mode (key) of the piece. If, for example, the tune was in E minor, then the accompanying instruments (bass, accordion, guitar, tsimbl) would play the E minor chord in the rhythm of the piece. Sometimes only one rhythm instrument would accompany the improviser. Then when the improvisation was finished he could signal to another musician to continue to improvise while he and others held the E minor rhythmic chord, or he could signal he was going back to the top of the tune, most likely to play it once more to the end. Then there were the display tunes, which were played usually as a solo or with one other instrument accompanying (tsimbl, bass, accordion, second violin, etc.). In these instances, the violinist would display his virtuosity to the wedding guests but particularly to the newlyweds and their parents. These semi-improvised tunes are the: *bazetsn* and *baveyen di kale*, doyne, moralne, *taksim, vulekhl,* and *zogetkhs* (cantorial recitative improvisations). The doyne, or in Romanian *doina* (often in the Mishebeyrakh mode), in the twentieth century became the cornerstone and most popular of all the semi-improvised display tunes played. The Romanian folk musicians (*lautare*) used the term to describe both vocal and instrumental melodies that either used a free or measured recitative form. Declamatory in nature, the singer or instrumentalist tried to wring out every level of human emotion from the elegiac doyne. Ironically, despite the doyne's lamenting quality, the highlight at a Jewish wedding in New York City from the 1920s–'50s was having either Naftule Brandwein or Dave Tarras play a doyne. Perhaps the beautiful doyne, replete with melancholy, represented the fortunate and unfortunate history of the Jewish people. Today the playing of at least one doyne in a klezmer concert is a must and is often the highlight of the performance. Violinists and clarinetists love to display their technical and improvisational skills while they sing the "Jewish blues." Here are the core dreydlekh, the vertebrae, of all klezmer music:

- The **glitshn** (Yiddish for "slippery, sliding areas") are portamenti. The violinist slides his finger (usually the first or second finger) from the lower note to the highest rapidly so that the intermediate notes are not defined. Occasionally the slides are executed from the high note to the lower note. The portamento along with the *krekhtsn* is used more than any other klezmer ornamentation.
- The **mordent** is a group of two or more grace notes played rapidly before the principal note. The mordent consists of the principal note itself and the note above or below. Mordents are used to give prominence to certain notes and musical phrases.
- The **krekhtsn** (Yiddish for "groans, moans") are the moaning, achy long notes that give klezmer music its distinctive sound, used usually by the violinist and clarinetist to evoke a momentary pulsating choked sob. This "hiccup" in the throat imitates the cantor's Ashkenazic singing style that was so prevalent prior to the Holocaust in Eastern Europe. In Western classical musical parlance the krekht (the cornerstone of all klezmer ornamentation) would be called an ap-poggiatura (Italian; meaning, a leaning note, a grace note, note of embellishment). On the violin it is created by playing the initial note, for example, the first finger, and then quickly flicking the higher note on the string with either the third or fourth finger while simultaneously suffocating the sound by pulling the down bow quickly and then suddenly stopping the bow at the tip. The note following the krekhts is played in another bow-stroke. The pitch of the krekhts, the hiccup of the grace note, is not important. There are some great klezmer musicians, like clarinetist Andy Statman, who perform the krekhts by leaning on the first note, stifling the second note, then accentuating and sometimes holding the third note. The use of krekhtsn is nearly unique to East European klezmer violin styles.
- The **kneytshn** (Yiddish for "fold, wrinkle, crease, crumple") are short notes with the achiness of the krekhtsn, but sometimes they are swallowed sharply as if squeezing the tip of the sound. Other times it is a slow krekhts momentarily flatted with a short downward portamento vanishing into thin air. This sharp, quick, downward movement is similar to a pull-off where the finger literally slides downward and pulls off the string as a kind of left-hand pizzicato. This is usually played with the fourth, third, or second finger.
- The **tshoks** (Yiddish for "lavishness, splendor, bluff, swagger") are "bent" notes (purposely not in concert pitch but just slightly under or over the actual note) with a laughlike sound that is more cackle than giggle. For example, this is a typical ending of a musical phrase in certain display melodies. After playing the descending phrase D, C-sharp B-flat, A as sixteenth notes, the third finger

would then play almost a C-sharp to almost the D-sharp, bending back and forth as three eighth notes and then landing finally on the dotted quarter D note. Dave Tarras sometimes called this ornament a *kvetsh* (Yiddish for "press, squeeze, pinch").

- The **turn** is an embellishment consisting of a group of rapid notes connecting one principal note with another, sometimes used to terminate a trill.

- The **harmonic** (sometimes called flageolet tones owing to the fact the sound made is similar to the flageolet flute) is the playing of a harmonic. Often harmonics are played at the end of a musical phrase or at the end of the tune. They are usually played with the second or third finger because the wider finger pads make it easier to lightly touch the string, creating the harmonic. By lightly touching the string at various notes, the violinist is able to play that same note one to two octaves higher. When employed during the middle of a melody the klezmer creates rapid whistling sounds that evoke etherealness.

- The **trill** (or **trillbrato** as I have coined it) is a combination quick trill and vibrato done at the same time. This creates a quivering sound. It can be played starting from the second, third, or fourth finger. The trillbrato begins with the upper auxiliary note. For example, the second finger plays a C, then a quick trill with vibrato begins with the third finger playing the C-sharp and resolves to the B-flat. The trillbrato is never longer than a quarter note and can be as short as an eighth note and used both in the middle or at the end of a music phrase. Among Roma violinists in the Carpathian Mountains, Transylvania, and Bessarabia they play a truer kind of trill but only very slow without the vibrato attached to it. It is played most often with the first or second finger and rarely with the fourth.

- The **ponticello** is the playing of the bow right next to the bridge. It creates a thin, squeaky, ethereal sound as if the klezmer violinist is playing on gossamer strings. In former times, it was used by some klezmers that played in the Carpathian Mountains and in Moldavia and Bessarabia. Today it is still used by some Roma musicians from these regions. With all of the thin overtones that are created, the sound resembles a kind of flute, like the exhaled breath heard from a Romanian pan flutist or Bulgarian *kaval* musician.

Figure 7.2   Examples of glitshn (portamenti) in klezmer music.

Figure 7.3 Examples of mordents in klezmer music.

Figure 7.4 Examples of krekhtsn with fingerings.

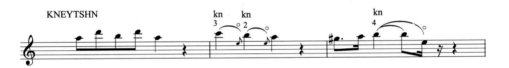

Figure 7.5 Examples of kneytshn with fingerings.

Figure 7.6 Examples of tshoks showing the microtonal nuance.

Figure 7.7 An example of a turn as played in klezmer music.

FLAGEOLET

Figure 7.8   The flageolet (harmonic).

TRILLBRATO

Figure 7.9   The trillbrato: trill and simultaneous vibrato.

PONTICELLO

sul ponticello

Figure 7.10   Ponticello (sul ponticello): bowing at the bridge.

When the violin was used as an accompaniment instrument (in Yiddish, *sekund*—"second" or *bratsh*—"viola") particularly in an ensemble composed of only strings (maybe a woodwind or two), then the musician kept the rhythm and harmony alone or in tandem with the bassist or cellist. Most sekund playing was with full bows, even pressure, and on the beat. If there was more than one accompanying instrument like a bass, then the sekund might play on the off beats. Some klezmer ensembles did not have bass, cello, trombone, or tsimbl, so a talented sekund player was required to keep the rhythmic energy as well as play clearly the chord changes. This was the case of Lajos Lelki who lived in Svajlava, Ukraine (Carpathian Mountains), who played sekund for a klezmer as well as a Roma band. In a wedding, a dance set could be a half hour or longer without stopping, thus playing sekund was physically challenging. Consequently musicians began to hold the violin vertically with their chin on the rib and the end pin jammed into their clavicle, bowing up and down (gravity helping) from head to toe rather than across the string from ear to ear. I witnessed a number of Roma musicians holding their violins like this while playing sekund for a *zhok* during my travels. Often the klezmers (Jewish or Roma) played a zhok as they accompanied the bride to the wedding canopy and the groom (who often came from another town) into the town to the synagogue. Sometimes this melody was known as a *krumer tants* (Yiddish for "crooked dance") since the bowing articulation made the cadence feel kind of limping. Some specifics to remember before you begin to play are:

- Alterations are an essential part of the klezmer style. Each time you play the tune it should not sound like a carbon copy of itself.
- Singing with the violin when you practice is essential. It will assist in all its facets and possibilities of bowing, fingering, intonation, tone control, speed, and precision. It will also inform you of the timbral possibilities and intricacies that you can seek in your violin playing.
- Embellishments will be determined by what genre the klezmer tune is, the tempo, and in which position you are playing.
- Ornamentation should be the spices you add to the main ingredients to help bring out and enhance the full robust flavors of the dish/melody and should never overpower the essential taste/notes.

SEKUND (for SLOW KHUSIDL or KHASIDIC NIGN)

Figure 7.11   Typical accompaniment pattern for the khusidl.

SEKUND (ZHOK)

Figure 7.12   Typical accompaniment pattern for the zhok.

SEKUND WALTZ

Figure 7.13   Typical accompaniment pattern for waltzes.

Figure 7.14 Typical accompaniment pattern for the freylekhs or skotshne.

Leopold Auer who was most responsible for transferring the klezmer's intensity and spontaneity into the Russian classical sound said about vibrato and portamento: The purpose of the vibrato, the wavering effect of tone secured by rapid oscillation of a finger on the string, which it stops, is to lend more expressive quality to a musical phrase, and even to a single note of a phrase. Like the portamento, the vibrato is primarily a means used to heighten effect, to embellish and beautify a singing passage or tone. Unfortunately, both singers and players of string instruments frequently abuse this effect just as they do the portamento, and by doing so they have called into being a plague of the most inartistic nature, one to which ninety out of every hundred vocal and instrumental soloists fall victim.[25] Then Auer characterized his philosophy on the use of embellishments:

This whole question of embellishment is an obscure one, and we have still to develop an authoritative body of rules which may serve as a guide to teacher and pupil. Now as in days gone by, the use of ornament in violin playing is taught in accordance with the individual teacher's point of view, and embellishments are played as the individual player's artistic good sense may dictate.[26]

I think of klezmer ornamentation as the great klezmer pianist Pete Sokolow told me when I interviewed him:

Once in the Catskills I was playing with Dave Tarras and Max Epstein happened to come by and hear me play. He dissected my style in five minutes. He said: "Listen, kid, the ornaments do not replace the melody, they only enhance the melody."[27]

Lastly this brings me to the subject of playing traditional klezmer music. First, when most people speak of playing traditional klezmer, the music they refer to is not older than the nineteenth century. In fact, klezmer music in Europe has been around since the development of Ashkenazic culture in the seventh century. The Jews moved eastward, and so too did their music. The indigenous music of each region where the Jews lived influenced the repertoire and style of playing of the Jewish musician while still maintaining its foot in the ancient Middle Eastern culture that gave birth to Judaism. Once the Jews stopped moving eastward, we began to see distinct styles of klezmer music being developed. By the seventeenth century, these styles were basically under two major genres (there were subgenres within these larger ones): the Polish-Ukrainian and the Romanian. Much of the klezmer repertoire was shared by so many people—Ukrainians, Polish, Romanians, Hungarian, Roma, Greek, etc.—that it's often difficult to hear the difference between the styles. Many ethnicities often claimed the same melody. Some experts will say that the 78-rpm records from before World War I are an excellent source of the klezmer sound of the last half of the nineteenth century, and they are. But what, for example, about the klezmer sound of Prague in the seventeenth century? Playing a zhok or a khusidl note for note with all the proper klezmer ornamentation is enough to perform the music on a cursory level, but as Dumitru Bughici[28] told me in 1985: "The music is much more than a flat two and sharp four."

What will make the klezmer music you play more authentic will be not only your being able to play your violin (or any other instrument) with the necessary klezmer ornamentation but your being able to move the audience with an emotional response; being able to tell the peripatetic history of the Jews in the diaspora through your instrument.

Figure 7.15   A khusidl from Berdichev.

Figure 7.16 A kolomeyke, played first as a hora/zhok then in traditional kolomeyke rhythm.

2

Figure 7.16   A kolomeyke, continued.

ZOGOT'S ZHOK

collected by Yale Strom from Motl Zogot,
who played it on the euphonium in his uncle's klezmer band
in his home town of Novozlatopil, Ukraine

Figure 7.17   A zhok from Novozlatopil, Ukraine.

BEN AVRAMENI

Figure 7.18 An original piece composed in traditional Moldavian klezmer violin style, by Yale Strom.

DISCOGRAPHY

Greenman, Steven, *Stempenyu's Dream: New Klezmer Compositions Written and Performed by Steven Greenman* (Greenfidl Music, 2004). Greenman plays original klezmer compositions that were inspired by the great klezmer violinist Stempenyu of Berdichev, Ukraine, and the great Jewish violin masters of Eastern Europe.

Schwartz, Leon, *Like in a Different World: A Traditional Violinist from Ukraine* (Global Village Music, 1995). Leon Schwartz (1901–1989) was a klezmer and classical music violinist who was born in Karapchiv, Ukraine (near Chernivtsi), and then lived in Queens, New York. He taught klezmer *bal-kulturnik* fiddlers Michael Alpert and Alicia Svigals. I personally visited him twice to take lessons from him as well as hear some of his stories about his childhood.

Strom, Yale, *Borsht with Bread, Brothers* (ARC, 2007). Strom performs tunes with his ensemble Hot Pstromi he collected in Eastern Europe rarely if ever heard in America. His playing combines both traditional ornamentation as well as a great deal of improvisation.

Strom, Yale, *Absolutely Klezmer, Vol. 2* (Transcontinental Music, 2008). Strom plays with his ensemble Hot Pstromi traditional klezmer tunes and some Yiddish songs.

Svigals, Alicia, *Fidl: Klezmer Violin* (Traditional Crossroads, 1997). Svigals, a fine klezmer violinist accompanied by an ensemble of some of the most noted klezmer musicians, today plays some of the more classic traditional klezmer tunes.

NOTES

1. *Bandura*: One version of this Ukrainian/Russian plectrum instrument looks like a mandolin with either a bulbous or flat back, and has six to eight strings. The other kind (sometimes called *bandora* or *Pandora)* is a zitherlike instrument with some seventy to eighty strings. There are no felt pads, and some even have frets. It is a difficult instrument to play.

2. *Cobza*: this Romanian plectrum instrument is related to the Arabic-Persian *oud* and was introduced to Romania by the Turks. It has four strings that are arranged in double courses, mainly in octaves (as dd, aa, dd, gg, though each player has his own tuning preference), and is picked by a quill robustly and rhythmically. It often provides percussive and chordal accompaniment to other instruments, usually the violin. In the Ukraine in the nineteenth century, blind minstrels were often called *cobzars* because the most common instrument among them was the cobza. Both the bandura and cobza are rarely seen, if ever, in klezmer bands in America and Europe today. I have seen the bandura played by Ukrainian peasants in Zmerinka (near Vinnicja), and I have see a Roma cobza player in a band in Botosani, Romania.

3. "Shulik Klezmer" in *Sefer Zikaron Le-kehilat Tomaszow Mazowiecki*, ed. M. Wajsberg (Tel Aviv: Tomasho organization in Israel, 1969), 333–34.

4. Interview with Felix Groveman (originally from the Bronx, New York) in Los Angeles, October 15, 1984.

5. Issacher Fater, *Yidishe Muzik in Polyn Tsvishn beyde Velt-Milkhomes* (Tel Aviv, Israel: Velt Federatsia fun Poylishe Yidn, 1970), 61.

6. Joachim Stutschewsky (1891–1982) was born in Romni, Ukraine, to a family of traditional klezmers. His father, Kalmen-Leyb Stutschewsky, was a klezmer clarinetist. He learned to play the fiddle at a young age and later switched to cello, traveling with the family klezmer band throughout the nearby villages and towns. Stutschewsky studied in Leipzig with Julius

Klengel and embarked on a richly varied musical career. In 1924 he moved to Vienna and helped found the legendary Vienna String Quartet along with Rudolf Kolisch. They became famous for premiering new works. While living in Vienna he was an active member, as composer, cellist, journalist, and organizer, of the Society for the Promotion of Jewish Music. In 1938 fleeing the Nazis, he moved to Switzerland and then that same year immigrated to Palestine. From the 1950s on, he devoted himself nearly exclusively to composing. In his compositions, Stutschewsky united modern classical music with elements of the folk music of Ashkenazi, Sephardic, and Yemenite.

7. The Brody Singers (sometimes called The Broder Singers) from Brody, Ukraine, were Jewish itinerant singers and actors who traveled extensively in the eastern region of Galicia in the Austro-Hungarian Empire, Romania, and Podolia, Ukraine, which was part of the Czarist empire. The first was Berl (Margolis) Broder (c.1815–1860). These semi-professional and professional Yiddish balladists sang and danced to locals' favorite songs and their own compositions in the beginning of the nineteenth century, often in comic disguises. Sometimes these songs and the dialogue in between them morphed into short one-act plays. The Brody Singers also found employment as *batkhonim* (traditional wedding bards), singers in cantors' choirs, and even klezmers. They were among the first to publicly perform Yiddish songs outside of the festival of Purim plays and Jewish wedding parties. The Brody Singers art became the antecedents of Yiddish musical theater. Eventually any singer who also performed a little skit in Yiddish was known as a Brody Singer whether or not he originated from Brody. It was in 1876 in Iasi, Romania, when the "father" of Yiddish theater, Abraham Goldfadn (1840–1908), after having seen a performance of a Brody Singer decided to put on with another actor, Shimen Mark, simple one-act plays in Yiddish in a wine garden called Pomul Verde (Rom for "green tree"). These skits spoke to the Jewish audience of their great and trying history. And thus Yiddish musical theater was born.

8. Joachim Stutschewsky, *Ha-Klezmorim Toldotehem OrakhHayehem v'Yezirotchem* (Jerusalem: Bialik Institute, 1959), 126–27.

9. Interview with Leopold Kozlowski (originally from Przemyslany, Ukraine) on November 11, 1984, in Krakow, Poland.

10. Ibid.

11. Zev Feldman, "Remembrance of Things Past: Klezmer Musicians of Galicia, 1870–1940," in *Polin: Studies in Polish Jewry, Vol. 16,* ed. Michael C. Steinlauf and Antony Polonsky, 29–57 (Oxford, England: The Littman Library of Jewish Civilization, 2003).

12. Interview with Leopold Kozlowski, see note 9 above.

13. Stutschewsky, *Ha-Klezmorim*, 124.

14. Stutschewsky, *Ha-Klezmorim*, 111.

15. The best violins in the world were made in Cremona, Italy: all violins since the seventeenth century have been judged against these incredible pieces of art. Of the various luthiers in Cremona in the late sixteenth and seventeenth centuries, these names stand above any others: Nicolo Amati (1596–1684), Guarneri del Gesu (1698–1744), and Amati's greatest and most famous pupil, Antonio Stradivari (c. 1644–1737).

16. Henry Sapoznik, *Klezmer! Jewish Music from Old World to Our World* (New York: Schirmer, 1999), 10.

17. Stutschewsky, *Ha-Klezmorim*, 115.

18. Sholem Aleichem, *Stempenyu*, in *Ale verk fun Shlem-Aleykhem* (New York: Sholem-Aleykhem Folksfond, 1919), 129.

19. Rarely the Yiddish word *shlayfer* would be used to mean the klezmer's musical ornamentation. In Yiddish this means to polish, sharpen, or whet.

20. Interview with Izu Gott (originally from Dorohoi, Romania) in Iasi, Romania, on August 15, 1981. Gott's original Yiddish was: "A sakh yidn hobn gefinen nekhome in Toyre limood, un di klezmer hobn aza nekhome geshafn zingendik di toyre."

21. Arno Nadel (1878–1943) was an accomplished arranger, composer, conductor, painter, poet, and playwright. He also became a collector of Jewish music and in the 1920s and 1930s compiled an anthology of synagogue and Eastern European Jewish folk music. In 1923 the Berlin Jewish community commissioned Nadel to compile and arrange new music for their liturgy. This resulted in a seven-volume manuscript compendium of synagogue music for cantor, choir, and organ, completed on November 8, 1938, one day before Kristallnacht. The anthology reflects Nadel's passion for collecting from the vast repertoire of Jewish music and features Eastern European folk and synagogue song, as well as cantorial music. Although Nadel was able to obtain an exit visa to England, he was too weak and dispirited to make the journey. On March 12, 1943, he was deported to Auschwitz concentration camp where he was murdered the same year. Before his deportation, Nadel left his entire library with a neighbor who managed to save a good part of the material. After the war, the neighbor returned it to Nadel's estate. Today it lies uncataloged in the Gratz College Archive in Philadelphia.

22. Abraham Zevi Idelsohn (1882–1938) was a prominent Jewish ethnologist and musicologist who conducted several comprehensive studies of Jewish music around the world. Idelsohn was born in Latvia and trained as a cantor. He immigrated to Palestine in 1905 and established a school of Jewish music there in 1919. In 1922 he moved to Cincinnati, Ohio, where he was a professor of Jewish music at Hebrew Union College. He is considered the father of Jewish ethnomusicology.

23. Stutschewsky, *Ha-Klezmorim*, 103.

24. Abraham Z. Idelsohn, *Jewish Music: Its Historical Development* (New York: Henry Holt, 1929), 24.

25. Leopold Auer, *Violin Playing as I Teach It* (New York: Lippincott, 1960), 22–24.

26. Mark Slobin, *Fiddler on the Move: Exploring the Klezmer World* (New York: Oxford University Press, 2000), 118.

27. Interview with Pete Sokolow in Brooklyn, New York, on May 14, 2009.

28. Dumitru Bughici (1921–2008) was a composer born in Iasi, Romania. He came from a family of well-known klezmer musicians. He played violin and accordion in his father's klezmer ensemble. Eventually he studied at the Conservatory in Iasi and became famous as a songwriter and classical composer. He often infused jazz motifs in his symphonic works. He emigrated to Israel in 1985.

8

Vocals

Elizabeth Schwartz

Of all instruments, there is only one with which we are born. We can learn to shape it and refine how we use it, but its timbre is wholly dependent on birth—and that is our voice. Whether we have a fine timbre or ear, everyone can and should sing—it's an intense expression of feeling and in that sense is the most personal musical activity. The voice is also the oldest of all instruments and in the case of Jewish music, where liturgy is chanted and sung (and not just spoken), singing has always been the most essential element of Jewish spiritual expression. It's important to note this fact, because early Jewish popular (i.e., non-liturgical) music—klezmer—was based on the chants of the synagogue, something early klezmer musicians certainly had heard all their lives.

In klezmer today, we are accustomed to hearing the modalities (scales) and ornamentation (bending and pinching notes, portamenti, repetition, etc.) of early cantorial music played by instruments like the clarinet and the violin. These instruments imitate the human voice. The klezmer vocalist, ironically, can learn from instrumentalists, copy these techniques, and reclaim the music for the voice. There are two particular ornamentations that form the cornerstone of klezmer instrumental performance, both of which came from the cantor: the bending downward of the note (*kneytsh*) and the breaking of the note (*krekhts*). So important is vocalization in the study of klezmer that many instrumental teachers will have their students sing the melodies before playing them (as violinist Steven Greenman would say, so as to "internalize" these melodies).

Today, there are many different styles of music that fall under the klezmer umbrella, and this presents many opportunities for different vocal styles. There is the *Khasidic nign* (wordless melody), the folk song, the bel canto art song, and American jazz style. So which style is the most legitimate? The answer is all of them. In this chapter, you will read about the history of these different styles and suggestions (where applicable) on how to sing them.

Regardless of style, there is one essential for the klezmer singer: facility with Yiddish. One needn't be fluent in Yiddish—or for that matter, read and write the *Alef Beys* (although it helps)—to begin singing klezmer, and there are different Yiddish dialects, all of which are legitimate (my own is the Romanian dialect I heard from my father's family).

Spoken Yiddish today has four basic sources: medieval German, Hebrew, Slavic tongues, and medieval Latin-based (Old French and Italian). Overall, the percentage of these sources probably breaks down as 80 percent Middle-High German, 10 percent Hebrew/Aramaic, 9 percent Slavic, and 1 percent medieval romance.

Originating in the Alsace-Lorraine region, Yiddish picked up vocabulary and dialects as Yiddish speakers migrated east: Western European Yiddish was spoken in Holland, Alsace-Lorraine, Switzerland, and most of Germany. There was a transitional Yiddish that was spoken in Bohemia, Moravia, Western Slovakia, and Hungary. The Yiddish of Eastern Hungary, Transylvania, and the Carpathian Mountains was influenced by the large immigration of *Khasidim* from Galicia. And lastly, the Yiddish that we associate with the great Yiddish writers like Mendl Mokher Sforim, I. L. Perets, Sholem Aleichem, et al., is Yiddish that developed in the nineteenth century in central Poland, southeastern Ukraine, and northeastern Lithuania. What we call Lithuanian Yiddish, or "Litvish," is spoken in Lithuania, Belarus, Latvia, northeastern Ukraine, and northeastern Poland. This Yiddish is considered the most cultured form, and this is the standard Yiddish taught at the university level around the world. Polish Yiddish, more commonly known as Galitsyaner, is spoken in the German-Polish frontier of 1939, central Poland, and in the western part of Galicia, which was part of the Austro-Hungarian Empire (Krakow being its cultural center). Finally, there is the Ukrainian, or what I call Romanian, Yiddish (Rumeynish), spoken in Eastern Galicia, Romania, and southeastern Poland. This dialect can be heard in the eastern part of the Carpathian Mountains, again due to the migration of the Khasidim from Podolia (a province of Ukraine).

What distinguishes these dialects from each other are vowel sounds and some minor differences in vocabulary and grammar. For the purposes of singing in Yiddish, one might sometimes sing in the dialect in which the song was written (for example, a World War I–era song like Yale Strom's "Getshinke," with lyrics from an anonymous poem of that era in Lithuania, should be sung in that dialect), but if you have a personal relationship with a dialect, you might choose to sing with that. Table 8.1 lists a few Yiddish words to indicate pronunciation.[1]

In any style of singing, the singer must be able to not only grasp but convey the true form and meaning of the lyrics. One well-known klezmer musician once told me, "I don't know any Yiddish, but I teach Yiddish singing." While it's true these are two separate issues, because there are distinct idioms to klezmer vocal technique, have you ever heard a foreigner sing in phonetic English? That's what any kind of phonetic singing sounds like. So a rudimentary facility is the minimum amount of Yiddish a klezmer singer needs (and the good thing is, the more you sing, the more your vocabulary and conjugation will be enhanced).

Table 8.1

English	Lithuanian	Polish	Ukrainian
To live	Lebn	Leybn	Leybn
Dowry	Nadan	Nadn	Nadn
Favor	Khesed	Kheysed	Kheysed
Candle	Likht	Lekht	Lekht
Wise	Klug	Klig	Klig
Of	Fun	Fin	Fin
Little	Kleyn	Klayn	Kleyn
Grace	Kheyn	Khayn	Kheyn
To Buy	Keyfn	Koyfn	Koyfn
To Build	Boyen	Boven	Boven
Sabbath	Shabes	Shabes	Shobes
Purim	Purim		Pirim

Music has been a vital part of Jewish culture since biblical times. Most of our information is about the ancient instruments (e.g., the *khatsotsera*—"trumpet," the *ugav*—"small flute," and the *kinor*—"lyre") and not the voice. But these instruments accompanied the choir when they sang in the temple. Abraham Idelsohn writes, "The singer was admitted to the choir at the age of thirty, and served up to fifty, the age when the decline of the voice began. Before his admittance, he had to have five years' training. In addition to the twelve adults, boys of the Levites were permitted to participate in the choir in order to add sweetness to the song."[2]

One can infer from this that not only musical ability but also knowledge and maturity were required to participate in the temple services. Eventually, non-Levites could play instruments in the services, but only Levites could sing. This was undoubtedly due to the necessity of text and the conveyance of spiritual tenets, requiring language. Thus, Idelsohn concludes, "the importance of music lies in the singing."[3]

After the destruction of the temple, the entire art of instrumental music playing by the Levites went with it. However, the singing of the psalms and the Torah, as well as recitation of the prayers, remained an essential aspect of devotion and was transplanted to the synagogue. The ancient Hebrews, not unlike their Semitic neighbors, drew inspiration for music from the local folk songs and folk songs of itinerant tribes. Thus we can surmise that even some of the holiest of the temple songs may have been borrowed from secular folk songs. "These Temple songs—folk tunes modified and sanctified—were in turn copied by the representatives of the people from all parts of the country who used to be present at the Temple service. They certainly learned the melodies together with the text and would carry them to their homes. Furthermore, many Levites would participate in public services in the synagogues and were naturally chosen to act as precentors, or leaders, in singing Psalms, portions of the Pentateuch and the Prophets."[4] From the days of the temple through the present, cantors, whether they were from the Khasidic or reform tradition, as well as klezmer instrumentalists, were inspired not only by the prayer melodies of the synagogue but by local folk music.

The earliest Jewish singers were influenced by the melismas and melodies they had heard in the synagogue. These melodies were transmitted orally, to be interpreted by each individual singer. (It would not be until the mid-1700s that European cantors would begin to read and write music.) The few manuscripts available were jealously guarded by the cantor because, besides his musical knowledge and vocal abilities, his worth depended on the demand among his congregants for specific compositions for prayers. For several centuries, the *nusakh* (Hebrew for "musical version") and the *trop* (Hebrew for "musical accent") were the only constant musical elements shared by the myriad synagogue chants of Western and Central Europe. The trops used in the Torah were composed between the sixth and ninth centuries BCE and reinterpreted by Ezra and Nehemiah and the Sanhedrin. We can't be certain if any of these early vocal styles exist today, but it is likely that the Yemenite and Babylonian Jews (Iraq, Iran) and even the Jews of the Caucusus today sing the purest form of these early synagogue melodies and vocal techniques (although even this has no doubt been corrupted by the influence of the indigenous cultures), because they were geographically isolated.

A great influence on the cantor's repertoire was the relationship between the Jews and their gentile neighbors in Western and Central Europe. Idelsohn writes,

> The close relations between Jews and gentiles in early centuries and especially during the reign of Charlemagne and his son Louis the Pious brought about a cultural reciprocity in which at first the Jews were more frequently those to exert the influence than those to be influenced. We learn this fact from the campaign which Bishop Agobard of Lyon, in his letters to Louis the Pious, started in 825 against the Jewish influence upon the Christians, which in his opinion endangered the Christian faith. He complains that . . . "Christians attend Jewish services and prefer the blessings and prayers of the Jewish rabbis; that Christians attend Jewish meals on the Sabbath and that Christians rest on the Sabbath . . ." In view of this fact, Agobard demanded that a prohibition should be issued to the effect that no Christian man or woman should attend Jewish services, nor observe the Sabbath, nor participate in Jewish festal meals, and that Christian people should stay away from the Jews.[5]

Eighteenth-century cantors were heavily influenced by Baroque instrumental music, and the melismatic qualities of the Semitic scales began to be replaced by minuets, gavottes, and other dance forms as settings for the most solemn prayers; the cantor in Europe before the days of the Emancipation had to make his music into something of a performance. In Eastern Europe, where the Emancipation came very late, the synagogue, in addition to being a house of worship, was a gathering place for Jews, their concert hall, opera house, recreational social hall, etc. The cantor provided the principal entertainment. He would try hard to move them to tears or to awe and admiration at the tricks and turns of his voice (no doubt by jumping octaves, glissandi, sustained notes, etc.).[6] The Jewish Enlightenment movement founded by German Jew Moses Mendelssohn (1729–1786) espoused that Jewish life and culture—including liturgical music—should be German, rather than Yiddish. The Semitic scales of the cantor were replaced by what was considered more progressive (i.e., more German and Christian sounding). Composer Louis Lewandowski (1821–1894) is considered one of the founding fathers of a more bel canto style of cantorial singing. Lewandowski introduced a more Western classical composition style for the prayers, ushering in a more operatic technique (four-part harmony for choirs, cantatas, etc.). The more elemental and natural sounds of the *bal-tfile* (Yiddish for "prayer leader") thus became more elevated and refined (and perhaps less spiritual).

Today, if you are an operatically trained singer, you can find comfortable bel canto stylistic choices in both cantorial singing and Yiddish art songs (similar to German lieder). There are distinctions between operatic and lieder singing, of course, primarily having to do with volume and timing—operas use full orchestras, while art song recitals can feature only piano accompaniment and acting. Operatic roles are character based, while an art song presentation requires no subsuming of the singer's own personality into a role. Moreover, an operatic aria is taken from a larger work, where an art song is usually a lyric poem set to music. During the eighteenth and nineteenth centuries, many rabbis frowned on cantors who sang prayers as operatic arias, but one can find myriad examples in the twentieth and twenty-first centuries of this practice. Alma Gluck recorded "Chanson Hébraïque" (accompanied by her husband, violinist Efrem Zimbalist), and it may be one of the best examples of this style. While clearly operatic in vocal technique, it is suggestive of Khasidic *davenen* (Yiddish for "prayer")—in Yiddish and Hebrew, Gluck employs the ornamentation of the cantor. Similar vocal technique can be heard in the cantorial singing of other classical purveyors of this form. Many of these artists recorded in Hebrew, French, Italian, English, and Yiddish, reflecting in language the different sources of the songs. The following exemplars were able to cross over from their cantorial roots to fame in the classical music world:

Yossele Rosenblatt (born Belaya-Tserkov in Ukraine, 1882–1933) was one of eleven children, and by the age of eight he was singing professionally, touring throughout the Austro-Hungarian Empire as a "boy wonder" cantor to the age of eighteen. His first cantorial posting was in Munkacs in 1900. His next posting was in Pressburg (Bratislava) in 1901 and five years later in Hamburg, where he served until 1912. This period had a profound influence on his singing style, as he tempered his more expressive and emotional delivery to suit the tastes of his German congregation. It was also here that he was introduced to opera—a style well suited to his magnificent timbre and four-octave range. Between 1907 and 1909 he recorded thirty-six albums, which helped to bring him worldwide recognition among Jewish and gentile audiences. He moved to America in 1912 and between his concertizing and cantorial duties, earned the soubriquet of "King of the Cantors." He tirelessly maintained his synagogue duties while recording and concertizing. He recorded his own compositions, as well as Hebrew and Yiddish songs. Wherever he performed, his repertoire always included cantorial selections, and he often turned down lucrative offers, notably from the Chicago Opera Company and Hollywood (in 1927 he turned down a $100,000 offer—an astronomical sum in those days—to appear in *The Jazz Singer*, although he did contribute off-screen vocals for a much smaller amount). He emigrated to Palestine in 1933 and tragically passed away three months later.[7]

As with Rosenblatt, **Jan Peerce** (born Yakob Perelmuth in New York, 1904–1984) began singing seriously at a young age: by nine years old, he sang in synagogue choirs, accompanying such noted soloists as Rosenblatt himself. As he pursued his cantorial training, he also played violin professionally (under the name of Pinky Pearl). In fact, there is an amusing anecdote of his performing with the great clarinetist David Tarras, who was dismissive when he learned that Peerce was interested in pursuing a career as a vocalist. Various agents gave Perelmuth less Jewish-sounding monikers like John Pierce, Paul Robinson, and Randolph Joyce (although he actually went in the other direction when he sang Jewish repertoire on WEVD, calling himself Jascha Pearl), but it was the great impresario Sol Hurok who gave him the name Jan Peerce. He continued to perform both operatically and liturgically, although he had no regular cantorial posting. When he retired from opera, he made the transition to Broadway, starring as Tevye in the 1971 *Fiddler on the Roof*. He continued to record until 1972.[8]

Born Rivn Ticker in New York, 1913–1975, **Richard Tucker** was born into a family of Romanian immigrants, who changed the family's last name to Tucker when he was small. Again, his musical aptitude was discovered at a young age, and he continued his cantorial training through high school. His most prestigious full-time posting to date was at the Brooklyn Jewish Center in 1943 (until then, he had to support himself as a salesman for the Reliable Silk Company). He married Sara Perelmuth (Jan Peerce's sister) in 1936. Whether or not due to professional rivalry, Peerce did not encourage his brother in-law's ambitions to follow in his footsteps, resulting in family friction. That said, he did introduce Tucker to operatic coach Zavel Zilberts, which was an important stepping-stone in Tucker's path to success. While Tucker failed the Metropolitan Opera House's "Auditions of the Air" in 1941, Met general manager Edward Johnson made a surprise visit to the Brooklyn Jewish Center to hear Tucker sing. Tucker was granted another audition and after that, a contract. He debuted in *La Gioconda*, a debut that ushered in a thirty-year career as the leading American tenor of the postwar era. He starred in operas all over the world (occasionally outshining costars like the young Maria Callas) and sang under Arturo Toscanini in the first full opera performance ever broadcast on national television (as Radames in *Aida*). His fame only continued to grow as a star of the Met. And he continued to officiate as a cantor on the High Holidays. He toured until his death in 1975.[9]

Often when classically trained singers sing in Yiddish, one can hear that operatic pronunciation, particularly in the rolling of the *R*. This isn't wrong, it's just formalized (and not how one would speak Yiddish). Yiddish is based on German, and the *R* is more guttural and back in the throat.

For the beginning klezmer singer, the easiest songs to sing are Khasidic *tish nigunim* (Yiddish for "table songs"), because a mastery of language (specifically, Yiddish) is not yet necessary. The Khasidim sing these songs of praise to reach a kind of spiritual adhesion to the Almighty (in Yiddish, *dveykes*), and in this sense, the intention of their singing is closest to that of the Levites, the singers of the first temple. The Khasidim sing *zmires* (Hebrew for "Sabbath songs") and nigunim (which can be in Hebrew, Yiddish, or without text) around the Sabbath table, at joyous events like weddings and circumcisions, and in the synagogue; today, many of these nigunim have been adopted by contemporary klezmer musicians. Primarily taught by ear and shared by the congregants, nigunim come close to being Jewish gospel; they are ecstatic songs of praise and worship. In the singing of nigunim, one can again hear the ornamentation of the klezmer. The congregation will sing nigunim as they pray aloud, reaching the end of the phrase in unison but with imperfect timing. This is particularly beautiful, as in beginning and ending in unison, the heterophonic singers convey community, but in individual phrasing, each singer conveys his own deeply personal experience. A perfect example of this heterophonic singing is "Mazl Tov/Mazel Tov," found on *Hassidic Tunes of Dancing and Rejoicing* (Various Artists, Folkways Records, 1978). The CD is predominantly vocal, but the great Israeli clarinetist (with whom I was fortunate to perform), Moshe Musa Berlin, is featured.

For singing a nign in a non-liturgical or concert environment, the reference to gospel is apt. When you have a number of singers all singing the same thing in unison, the lead vocalist can and should augment and differentiate the melody. When singing a nign with my bandmates and (hopefully) the audience, I will set the melody for the others and then harmonize. If there is a strong enough base from the other singers and musicians, I will also syncopate and improvise. It's all about layering.

Sometimes, the singers of nigunim are singing psalms, but sometimes they aren't singing any words. If the Khasidim aren't singing text with nigunim, what are they singing? They are singing repetitive syllables. "The Galitzyaner Hassidim (Modzitz, Ger, Bobov) favored the 'typical' vocables like Bim-Bam, Ya-Ba-Bam, Dai-Dam (especially Bim-Bom around Moditz and Yadi-Yadi in Ger); Lubavitchers liked the more liquid Na-Na-Na, Ni-Nam, Ma-Ma-Ma or Oy-Yoy; and Hungarian/Carpathians had a more tragic outlook with a lot of Oy-Oy, Doy-Doy . . ."[10] Add to this the Vishnitser Khasidim, who sing vay-vay-vay.

For an example of a Khasidic nign, I recommend the Gerer nign also known as "Ki Onu Amekha." The lyrics are pronounced in an Ashkenazic (or Yiddish-accented) Hebrew.

Khasidim, as well as Orthodox Jews, follow Talmudic rules of *tsnius* (Yiddish for "modesty") very seriously, and among these is the prohibition against listening to a woman sing. "Kol Ishah" is derived from the Song of Solomon: "Let me hear your voice, for your voice is sweet and your face is beautiful." With the prohibition, the concern is that listening to a woman's voice will stir sexual desire. But there is a great deal of debate about how strenuously to follow this prohibition. Some hold that a grown man can never listen to a woman sing, others that they can't listen to a woman's voice while studying Torah or reciting the *Sh'ma*. Later authorities of Jewish law have gone so far as to debate whether the prohibition applies to a recorded voice. (I recorded with the great klezmer clarinetist-mandolinist Andy Statman, who felt more comfortable laying down his tracks after mine had been already recorded.) When it comes to the singing of nigunim or zmires, women are generally permitted to sing in a group, so long as no individual voice stands out.

There was one select group of women singers who not only defied this prohibition (to the extent possible in the 1910s and '20s) but their extraordinary vocal abilities, deep spirituality, and mastery of cantorial ornamentation put them in the class of the best male cantors: the *Khazentes* (Yiddish for "female cantors"). These women demonstrated not only technique but a deep love and dedication to their craft, and because they would never have been permitted to lead services, also showed a certain degree of forward-thinking moxie for daring to sing *khazones* (Yiddish for "cantorial music"). The Khazentes often sang in their lowest chest registers, perhaps because sounding more like a man made their music less shocking. Sophie Kurzer from Odessa may have been the first woman to record khazones. Some of the other notable Khazentes sang pseudonymously, like Shaindele di Khazente (née Jean Gornish) and Bas Sheva (née Bernice Kurzman), but some dared to use their own names, like Perele Feig (possessed of an astonishingly androgynous timbre) and Fraydele Oysher, daughter of legendary Yiddish Avenue actor Moishe Oysher; so great was Fraydele's love of khazones that she had cantorial music written for her to sing on the Second Avenue stage, since she could never have sung it in synagogue. No study of cantorial singing (or, in my opinion, any Jewish singing) is complete without listening to the works of the Khazentes.

From my own perspective, the prohibition of Kol Ishah has been applied somewhat fluidly. There have been a number of Hot Pstromi concerts for orthodox audiences that excluded me. But years ago, during a concert at the Brooklyn Public Library, there were several Khasidic men in attendance. In deference to them, I took my time announcing the song I was about to sing, so as to give them time to leave the room. Not only did they stay, they danced ecstatically. Similarly, at a concert I gave in Jerusalem, Haredi men not only stayed while I sang, some of them even took up instruments to play along with me (which delighted me, as secular Israelis in the audience had never seen such a thing). There is a point here: just as klezmer music came from Jewish cultural and religious life, it is sensitive and legitimate for the singer (as well as the instrumentalist) to understand the context for the music and the listener. It's also well worth mentioning Rashi's commentary on the Babylonian Talmud (Berakhot 57b [c.1100]): "The sweet voice of a woman . . . can restore a man's spirit." My happiest experience with the ban of Kol Ishah was in its breaking; on March 18 of 2012, I became the first female vocalist in 125 years to sing before a mixed audience in the magnificently restored landmark Eldridge Street Synagogue on New York's Lower East Side.

Early singers of Hebrew and Yiddish song benefited from a lifelong familiarity with Jewish liturgy, but they weren't only cantors or *bale-tfiles* (Yiddish for "prayer leaders"). Beginning in the eleventh century, itinerant Jewish singers began to entertain the public. Called by many names (*shpilman*—"musician" in Yiddish, *lets*—"jester" in Hebrew, and *nar*—"fool" in Yiddish), these entertainers played music and sang comical and improvised songs based primarily on their knowledge of the Talmud, Torah, and daily synagogue prayers. They became popular fixtures at Jewish weddings, providing merriment and sometimes filling the same role as the cantor (to the dismay of the cantors and the rabbis). By the seventeenth century, these wedding bards (and sometimes also instrumentalists) were more commonly referred to as *batkhns*.

The batkhn's wedding duties developed to the point where he was generally the master of ceremonies and helped to prepare the bride, beginning with musically accompanying her to the *mikve* (Yiddish for "ritual bath"), the *bazetsn* (Yiddish for "the seating," where the bride was entertained as her closest female friends and relatives came to pay their respects and, generally, where her hair was shorn), leading to the *baveynen* (Yiddish for "the crying"). It was during this last preparation that the batkhn would display his extensive knowledge of Talmud, vocal, and intellectual skills by singing a long, a cappella, improvised poignant song, in rhyme, exhorting the bride to weep along with her guests. The batkhn continued his wedding duties during the wedding party, sometimes singing an unaccompanied display piece both in rhyme and non-rhyming verse, both with great poignancy and sincerity and with scathing (and sometimes, ribald) wit. He would honor the bride and groom, comment on the wedding presents and the guests, and would not hesitate to embarrass anyone who hadn't given generously. Table 8.2 is an example of *batkhones* (the batkhn's improvised song).[11]

By the late nineteenth century, batkhns, as well as itinerant Jewish minstrel singers from Brody, Ukraine, known as Broder Singers, would perform songs to entertain audiences. In fact, the Broder Singers were thought to have inspired Avram Goldfadn

Table 8.2

Yiddish	English
Oyb ir hat a tokhter a shlak,	If you have a daughter who is a nuisance
Tah kumt tsu undz in der yeshiva	Then come to us in the *yeshiva*
Ir vet patur veryn fun dem pak	You will dispose of this bundle
On sheloshim un on sheva	Without thirty and seven.
Dah kent ir oysklaybn	There you can choose a yeshiva student
A bokher mit a ale meyles	With all the virtues,
Vos ken lernen un shraybn	One who learns and writes and even
Un afile paskenen shayles.	Rules on ritual questions.
Koyft im nor shtivl mit kalashn	Buy him boots and galoshes
Un git I nor smetene mit khale,	And give him only sour cream on challah
Dertsu nokh a por groshn—	In addition, a few *groshn*—
Gefelt im shoyn di kale	Now he's pleased with the bride

(1840–1908) to create Yiddish musical theater.[12] The Broder Singers were colorful and flamboyant and performed songs and monologues that they often composed themselves. They were the first professional actors in the Yiddish theater. What sets the Broder Singers apart from cantors and batkhns is that their repertoire and frame of reference was usually secular.[13] With the widening influence of the Enlightenment came a certain level of freedom for Jews, who no longer feared rabbinical prohibitions against attending these performances, which often occurred in wine cellars and cafés. The first prominent Broder Singer was Ber Margoles (1815–1868), who called himself Berl Broder. So significant was his body of work that the term "Berl Broder" became generic for all singers of this style. Some of Berl Broder's original songs, along with the works of his son and grandson who continued the tradition of secular Yiddish writing, can be found in his grandson Ber Margulies' book *Dray Doyres Lider Fun Berl Broder* (Yiddish for "Three Generations of Songs from Berl Broder"). While Berl Broder was unschooled in liturgy and cantorial technique, some subsequent Broder Singers, like Vevl Zbarzher (approximately 1826–1883) and Eliakum Zunser (1836–1913), were also renowned batkhns and helped to raise the art form to a more respected level.

The idioms of the Cantor have remained a constant in the development of klezmer. As European Jews migrated east, their music was influenced by their host countries, resulting in the Polish-Ukrainian and Romanian styles. The repository for this mixing, exchanging, and borrowing of Greco-Turkish tunes was the Moldavian/Bessarabian region of Romania.[14] This is the region that gave klezmer musicians and vocalists the *doyne.*

From the nineteenth century to the eve of World War II, klezmers performed display pieces for the bride and groom's table. Generally, the clarinetist or violinist would play as poignantly and evocatively as possible, using the modal scales, repetition, and chord modulation of the cantor, building the emotion almost to the breaking point before then segueing into an upbeat *freylekhs, khusidl,* or *bulgar.* The soloist guided the emotions of the wedding party while, at the same time, showcased his virtuosity and improvisational talent while his bandmates held down a steady drone (sustained chord) underneath his playing. While the klezmer doyne has no set form, it has an expressive vocal quality (again, in imitation of the voice), often referencing Jewish prayer. The most typical instruments of the doyne are violin, clarinet, and *tsimbl* (also called cimbalom or hammered dulcimer). Usually, the soloist will begin in one key, modulating to build tension, and conclude back in the original key. And while some doynes are complete unto themselves, it is common, as with the weddings above, for the soloist to lead into an upbeat, merry tune to help release the emotional tension that was built up in the doyne. Ethnographer Marc Slobin writes,

> The Romanian klezmer doyne is a rubato, semi-improvised melody that is the cornerstone of Romanian klezmer repertoire. In this listening piece, the klezmer showed off his virtuosity through improvisation and fioritura, imitating the coloratura of the cantor. Often, the doyne told the folk tale of a shepherd's grief upon finding that he had lost his flock, and how he took out his panflute and played this lament.[15]

Slobin's description of the klezmer doyne includes references to shepherds and flocks that seem anachronistic to Eastern European Jewish life. In Russia and most of Eastern Europe, Jews were historically forbidden to own land, let alone farm it (there were a small percentage of Jews in the Carpathian Mountains who were the exception to this rule). So where do these pastoral images come from? The answer lies not only in the Romanian folk tradition of the doyne but in the audiences for klezmer music. Often, Jewish musicians performed for gentile audiences—and the universal and eternal rule for all musicians, then as today, is to give the audiences whatever they want. And when a klezmer found himself performing for Romanians, he was sure to play Romanian doinas, in the Romanian style, to please his listeners.

In style and influence, the instrumental Romanian doina bears all the hallmarks of the Turkish *taksim*. Even the shepherd's lament bears distinct similarities to the Turkish shepherd's traditions. While some contemporary Romanian scholars grudgingly acknowledge a general "Oriental" influence (be it Turkish or Middle Eastern) on this Romanian folk tradition, it is notable that the areas where the Romanian doina was most prominently performed were also those areas where the Turkish influence was the greatest; Romania did not gain its independence from the Ottoman Empire until 1877, relatively recently in history.[16] (I have sung a Yiddish doyne all over Romania and have been warmly received by Jewish and gentile audiences. This reaction to the doyne seemed to derive primarily from their pleasure that I was singing "their" music, even when the lyrics were in Yiddish.)

The instrumental klezmer doyne will generally segue into an upbeat freylekhs, but the vocal doyne shares more with its Romanian cousin—the song is all. In the case of the doyne that I call "Doyne din Targu Frumos" (aka, "Doina" by Barditcher; my ancestors came from Targu Frumos, a town in Moldavia 30 kilometers West of Iasi, hence the title), I first familiarized myself with the melody line, in tempo, as written. And while I initially recorded it as written, in subsequent years I have elaborated on that version because, for me, the true form for singing a doyne should be in the style of doyne performance. Free meter is a luxury for a singer because (just as in prayer) you can take as much time as you wish getting to the end of each phrase. Practice singing over a droned (i.e., sustained) minor chord and adding your own ornamentation. Don't lose the melody line in favor of showing off your grace notes. Fioratura is a hallmark of the doyne, but it's important not to "over soul" (to borrow a phrase from contemporary pop singing). There aren't too many singers today who are singing the doyne as if it were an instrumental piece, so I recommend Romanian director Radu Gabrea's film *Romania, Romania: Searching for Schwartz*. This is a chronicle of a tour I did in Romania and in which I sing the doyne as described here.

Klezmer in Europe, particularly in the twentieth century, not only included the above styles but also the phenomenon of Polish Yiddish cabaret (a natural evolution of the performances of the Broder Singers). In Warsaw, there were myriad clubs that presented musical skits (largely from preexisting repertoire from Europe and America) and five theaters devoted to Yiddish culture. These music revues were unique, because they brought much-needed art to Jewish audiences. Beginning in the 1920s, *kleynkunst* (Yiddish for "small art") cabarets became popular among the Polish Jewish cognoscenti. A typical program included skits, monologues, Rom music, art songs about Jewish life (both dramatic and satirical), and political satire performed by actors, musicians, and singers. These performances drew from past and contemporary Yiddish writers. Under Nazi occupation, the repertoire expanded to support and laud the bravery of Jews who resisted, sympathized with those Jews who were victimized, and criticized those Jews seen as collaborating. Beloved folk songs like "Rozhinkes Mit Mandln" (Yiddish for "Raisins and Almonds") and "Papirosn" (Yiddish for "Cigarettes") were given sardonic new interpretations—in the case of the former, "Nisht Keyn Rozhinkes, Nisht Keyn Mandln" (Yiddish for "No Raisins and No Almonds") and for the latter, the macaronic "Nishtu keyn Przydziel" (Yiddish and Polish for "There Are No Food Coupons")—about the corruption of Chaim Rumkovski, leader of the Lodz ghetto. There were also significant kleynkunst cabarets outside of Warsaw, in Lodz, Vilne, Bucharest, and other cities with large populations of intellectual, cultured, and avant-garde Jewish performers and audiences.

In 1904, the Yiddish theater impresario Avram Goldfadn emigrated from Iasi, Romania (where he created the first Yiddish musical theater) and settled in New York. He is credited as the "father" of the Second Avenue Yiddish theater. His prolific output of serious plays, poems, and songs included the operetta *Shulamis* (which gave us the song "Rozhinkes Mit Mandln") and even "Tsu Dayn Geburstog"—the happy birthday song in Yiddish. But more importantly, it spawned a tradition of Jewish musical theater and vaudeville and gave us wonderful composers and their songs from the 1910s through the 1930s: Sholem Secunda ("Bay Mir Bistu Sheyn"), Abraham Ellstein ("Oi, Mame, Bin Ikh Farlibt," "Abi Gezunt"), Joseph Rumshinksy ("Alte Liebe," "As Ikh Ken Keyn Mame Nisht Zeyn"), and Alexander Olshanetsky ("Mayn Shteytle Belz," "Ikh Hob Dikh Tsufil Lib"). One show in 1909 gave us the joyous wedding song "Khusn Kale Mazeltov" (Yiddish for "Congratulations to the Bride and Groom"), now a standard at any Jewish wedding with a klezmer band.

I have heard songs from the Second Avenue repertoire performed in both bel canto and in the jazz standard style. There is no wrong way to sing them, but the songs themselves as well as the performance templates indicate that these are the precursors to the Broadway standard. The most important skills needed to sing them well are good Yiddish pronunciation, emotive ability, and a trained voice. Some of the stars of the Second Avenue Yiddish theater were Molly Picon, Boris and Bessie Tomashefsky, Jacob Kalich, Moishe Oysher, Ida Kaminska, Lillian Lux, Pesach Burstein, Seymour Rexite, and many other great artists, including two wonderful women I had the pleasure to meet before they passed away: Shifra Lehrer and Mina Bern.

As has always been the case with musical theater, many songs have been lifted from shows and become standards in their own right—and many of these songs can swing. Singing in the jazz style (e.g., a standard like "Bay Mir Bistu Sheyn," one of the greatest Jewish crossover songs of all time) invites the singer to practice vocalese, or vocal improvisation. The primary distinction between improvising in jazz and improvising in klezmer is that a jazz improvisation is done over the song's form with all the chord changes, but in klezmer the improvisation is generally done over a single chord, in most cases, a minor one. Both styles require complete familiarity with the scales, and there are simple basic steps for preparing your own klezmer vocalese.

The following suggestions for developing improvisational technique can also be applied to warming up before singing. First and foremost, listen to and practice singing the scales. This is not only the best way for a singer to memorize and internalize the notes of the scales, it is also a great way to warm up your vocal chords. (See the notated scales in the "Violin" chapter of this work.)

Once you feel comfortable with the scales, it's time to practice improvising over a minor chord. Don't set a time limit for yourself; sing along to the chord for ten minutes (or longer). Spend that time not only running up and down the scales but experimenting. Jump an octave (both up and down), bending the notes and using glissandi. Throw in cantorial ornamentation. Borrow some melody lines that may seem anachronistic but fit within the chord structure, and syncopate your timing within the phrase. Aside from staying in key, there are no rules, and it's better for the purposes of practicing to hit a few bad notes than to be tentative. Once you feel comfortable with this, try to improvise over the entire form, with chord changes, of a standard like "Bay Mir Bistu Sheyn" or "Sheyn Vi Di Levone" (which is almost the identical form).

You can even substitute the traditional scatting syllables with those in the Khasidic nign style. Many singers (myself included) mastered the krekhts through listening and repetitive imitation, but for the purposes of this chapter I asked cantor Leon Natker how he would technically describe it. His suggestions: Keep your palate up, tongue down, and throat relaxed. While moving as much air as possible through your diaphragm, let the palate slip down. You must support this throughout, using your diaphragm and not your throat. Similarly, to pinch off the note (the *kneytsh*), you must also control the air with your diaphragm and not your throat. The closest descriptive I can use for the kneytsh is it's like a hiccup at the end of a sob (which is why it conveys that plaintive quality). You can work within these parameters to develop your own distinct style for singing klezmer music.

One of the earliest proponents of the crossover from Yiddish repertoire to American jazz was Al Jolson (1886–1950). Best known for starring in the first talkie, *The Jazz Singer* (1927), by the 1930s Jolson became the most successful and highest paid singer in America. "Jolson was to jazz, blues, and ragtime what Elvis Presley was to rock 'n' roll."[17] Sisters Clara (1923–) and Minnie (1925–1976) Bagelman found phenomenal success when they changed their names to Claire and Merna Barry. The Barry Sisters ("the Jewish Andrews Sisters") were prominent American artists through the 1940s to 1960s, appeared on *Ed Sullivan* and *Jack Paar*, starred in the Yiddish radio show *Yiddish Melodies in Swing*, and even performed behind the Iron Curtain in 1959, one of the rare American acts to tour through the USSR. They recorded eleven albums, including popular American songs like "Raindrops Keep Falling on My Head," translated into Yiddish!

And as is the case with every style of klezmer instrumental, new songs are being written today in the old style as well as the new. An example of a contemporary jazz vocal piece, "Café Jew Zoo," with words and lyrics by Yale Strom (recorded by Hot Pstromi), was deliberately written in an older jazz style.

And finally, as klezmer is the music of a people, we come to one of the most common styles: folk music. By the end of the Middle Ages, Christian liturgical music had moved from plainsong to polyphonic melody, while secular music and song became more accessible to the masses. Although the Jews were forced to live in ghettos, these changes influenced them, too. Among the Christians, secular music and song were represented by wandering troubadours, minstrels, minnesingers, *spielleut,* and jongleurs who entertained both at the courts of the aristocracy and in markets across Europe. But two of the most famous Provençal troubadours of the thirteenth century were Jews: Bonfils de Narbonne and Charles le Juif. Among the German Jews, the minnesinger Susskind von Trimberg (born around 1220 in Trimberg, near Wurzberg) was the best known, often satirizing in song the gentiles' anti-Semitism. Traveling from town to town and castle to castle, these wandering minstrels endured hardships and abasements. One gets a sense of Susskind's pain from a song he wrote: "I want to grow a beard, long must it be, its hair quite gray. And then I'll go through life the way, the Jews have always gone . . . wrapped in a cape, billowy and long: Deep under the hat hiding my face; Meek and with a humble song; bare of God's grace."[18]

The lyrics of these itinerant entertainers were taken from biblical themes and homilies. The early Jewish minstrels acted as go-betweens, disseminating popular gentile vocal and dance melodies that the local cantors then incorporated in the Sabbath services. The cantors also took the music fashions of the ghetto to the outside world. For most Jews in the thirteenth and fourteenth centuries, life in these ghettos was difficult. Jews were governed by strict regulations, especially when they worked, often in hostile conditions outside the ghetto walls. After a hard week, they sought respite in the synagogue service and to the great dismay of the rabbis, often demanded that the cantor sing his prayers to the gentile tunes they had heard outside the ghetto walls. Fearful that the singing of gentile music was contaminating not only the synagogue service but the ethics and morals of Jewish life, the rabbis in Western and Central Europe, one by one, began to ban the playing of any kind of music and the singing of Christian melodies in the synagogue. Some cantors followed these restrictions but others were swayed by their congregants—and some were banished from their communities and forced to wander from city to city, leading prayers and concertizing wherever they could.

The earliest documented Ashkenazic Jewish folks songs were collected by Eisik Walich of Worms in the late sixteenth century.[19] What differentiated these songs was not just that the lyrics weren't in Hebrew but accordingly that the lyrics didn't contain religious motifs. Jewish folk songs from the sixteenth century onward were primarily in the language spoken by Jews outside of the synagogue and dealt with secular issues (love, Jewish holidays, and social life). Just as Jewish culture adopted aspects of the host countries, so too did the klezmers adopt folk music to their repertoire. A good case in point is the Yiddish song "Lustig Zayn" (aka, "May Ofes," "Reb Dovidl"). I recorded this (as well as other traditional Yiddish songs) on the ARC UK recording *The Devil's Brides*. "Lustig Zayn" had been a Polish folk melody, which klezmers began playing and reinterpreting with their ornamentation. There's a great apocryphal story that Frédéric Chopin urged his fellow Poles to stop singing the song because the klezmers had made it sound too Jewish. Whether or not this ever happened, it is illustrative of the notion that one can add klezmer musical idioms to a folk song and make it sound Jewish. To sing klezmer in the folk style, one must again harken back to the vocal traditions of the synagogue—not because the songs are liturgical, but because these ornamentations have become an indelible part of the music's performance. If one is singing Celtic folk music, there are certain idioms that would be distinct to that style, as with the distinct folk styles of any country and region. As klezmer music is now performed around the world, it is not necessary to adhere closely to an Eastern European style of singing, but bringing klezmer technique to your performance can only enhance and authenticate your performance and makes the song distinct from other styles. So too can the singer, regardless of background, maintain the song's Jewish character, nuance, and soul. And whether or not we think of the days of the first temple when we sing, we can reclaim this music with our voices.

Figure 8.1   "Ki Onu Amekho" (Hebrew for "We Are Your People"), a Gerer nign originally from Gora Kalawaria, Poland.

Figure 8.2 Buhusher nign originally from Buhusi, Romania.

Figure 8.3 Buhusher nign originally from Buhusi, Romania, with vocal harmony and improvisation.

Figure 8.4 "Café Jew Zoo," music and lyrics by Yale Strom.

Lyrics for "Ki Onu Amekha," a Gerer Khasidic nign originally from Gora Kala-waria, Poland, are listed in table 8.3, and lyrics for "Café Jew Zoo," composed and written by Yale Strom, are listed in table 8.4.

Table 8.3

Yiddish	English
Ki awnu amekha, v'atah eloheynu	We are your people and you are our ruler
Awnu v'nekhah v'atah awvinu	We are your children and you are our parent
Awnu avahdekha v'atah adoneynu	We are your servants and you are our sovereign
Awnu keh-ha lekha v'atah khel keynu	We are your community and you are our portion
Awnu nakha la sekha v'atah goraleynu	We are your heritage and you are our destiny
Awnu so nekha v'atah roheynu	We are your flock and you are our shepherd
Awnu khar mekha v'atah note reynu	We are your vineyard and you are our tender
Awnu feh'oolasekhah v'atah yotesreynu	We are your creatures and you are our creator
Awnu raya sekha v'atah doh deynu	We are your faithful and you are our dear one
Awnu seghula sekha v'atah kihroveynu	We are your treasure and you are our near one
Awnu amekha v'atah malkeynu	We are your people and you are our ruler
Awnu ma-a-mi-rekha v'atah m-a-mi-reynu	We are your chosen and you are our chooser

Table 8.4

Yiddish	English
Ikh hob shpatzirt oyf di shtile gasn	I've walked down the quiet streets
Der vind hot geblozt der regn gegosn	As the wind blows and the rain pours
In mayn alte zikhroynes, shmek ikh nokh di halobtsis	In my own memories, I taste the hot stuffed cabbage,
Dem tam fun di shvemlekh mit kasha,	the mushrooms with kasha,
un trink-zikh di biter mashke	And drink the bitter whiskey.
Plutsem, demalt farshtipt in a vinkl	Suddenly, around the corner,
Shteyt a meydl in a rekl	stands a woman in a coat.
Zi bet mir kum-zhe arayn	She asks me to come
In dem Café Jew Zoo far a gleyzele vayn	inside Café Jew Zoo for a glass of wine.
(Chorus)	
Kum free, un blayb biz shpeyt	Come early and stay late
Tants-zikh der Yidish tret	Dance the Jewish step
Mir hoodoo, un voodoo,	We hoodoo and voodoo
Bay der Café Jew Zoo	At the Café Jew Zoo.
Der klezmer shpilt a shtark, gutn fidl	The klezmer plays a strong, good fiddle
Un di sarvers zingn a Yidish lidl	And the waiters sing a Yiddish song
Mentshn zingn, tantsn, raykhern un shvitzn	People sing, dance, smoke and sweat
Zeyr tsitsis, kapotes, shaytln flutern	Their *tsitsis*, *kapotes* and wigs flapping.
Di luft shmekt fun leydik zikhroynes	The air smells from empty memories
Zer shmeykhln zenen vi eybik shmanzes	Their smiles feel like timeless nonsense
Dos meydl in der sheyne rekl	The woman in the beautiful coat
Kumt tsu mir mit a kleyn pekl	Comes to me with a small package.
(Chorus)	
Zi nemt mayn hent, mir tantsn, mir kushn zikh	She takes my hands, we dance, we kiss
Di musik, ir reyekh, alts is fahrvisht	The music, her scent, everything is a blur.
Ikh gedenk nokh di melodia fun mayne kinder yorn	I remember the melodies from my childhood
Bobe hot gezungn, un der Zeyde hot geblozt	Grandma sang and Grandpa blew.
In dem pekl, farpokt mit papirn,	In this package, wrapped with paper,
Leygt-zikh a talis v'flekt mit treyrn	Is a *talis* stained with tears.
Ver zaynen di mentshen, mit zeyr modne punimer?	Who are these people, with their curious faces?
Zey tshepn-zikh, kvetshn-mikh, zey zogn ikh tehilim	They bother me, they pinch me, they say psalms.
(Chorus)	
Is dos benkenshaft, oder iz dos shuld?	Is this nostalgia, or is this guilt?
Is dos Semoyl farshtelt vi Shmul?	Is this Samael disguised as Solomon?
(Chorus)	

SUGGESTED RECORDINGS

Theo Bikel, *Treasure of Yiddish Theatre and Folk Songs* (Rhino Handmade, 2004). From one of the masters of Yiddish song, this compilation by Theo Bikel gives a broad sense of traditional Yiddish folk song. A consummate actor, Bikel tells a story with each song.

Yale Strom & Hot Pstromi, *Borsht with Bread, Brothers* (ARC Music UK, 2007). The glissandi in "Vemn Veln Mir Dinen, Brider" (Yiddish for "Whom Shall We Serve, Brothers") were actually notated in the music; "Ki Onu Amekha" is a psalm and is sung in a more liturgical style; "Ver Es Ken Keseyder Tseyln" (Yiddish for "Who Can Count in Order") has improvisational vocal breaks in the cantorial style of the batkhn.

Yale Strom & Hot Pstromi, *Café Jew Zoo* (Naxos World Records, 2000). The title track is a contemporary jazz composition/arrangement that has an almost Brecht-Weill feel and is a combination of klezmer and swing, with Yiddish vocals in a jazz style.

Yale Strom & Hot Pstromi, with Miriam Margolyes, *The Devil's Brides: Music from "The Witches of Lublin"* (ARC Music UK, 2011). The world of this recording was eighteenth-century Poland, and I sing in the appropriate Polish dialect. As the entire CD was recorded in one session (and with one take, except where I tripled the harmony on "Lishuasekho"), there is a rawness and spontaneity to the vocals. Note the Ashkenazic Hebrew on "Lishuasekho."

Various artists, *Great Cantorial Singers: Female Voices of the Golden Age of Chazzanut* (Tara Publications, year n/a). This is the only recording of the extraordinary Khazentes, who broke the barrier of women singing liturgy; note the androgyny of some of the timbres. During a time when there were no female cantors, this music was recorded years before women would officially lead prayers in synagogue for all the congregants.

Various artists, *Hassidic Tunes of Dancing and Rejoicing* (Folkways Records, 1978). This compilation CD provides some wonderful examples of heterophonic and ecstatic Khasidic singing. Moreover, it is a rare field recording of music that might not otherwise have been available to outsiders.

SUGGESTED READING

"Development of Yiddish over the Ages: Yiddish Dialects," JewishGen.org, http://www.jewishgen.org/databases/givennames/yiddial.htm (accessed September 7, 2011).

James A. Drake, *Richard Tucker, A Biography* (New York: Dutton Adult, 1984).

Judith Kaplan Eisenstein, *Heritage of Music: The Music of the Jewish People* (New York: Union of American Hebrew Congregations, 1972).

Robert Garfias, "The Romanian Doina," Passion Discs, http://www.passiondiscs.co.uk/articles/doina.htm.

Abraham Z. Idelsohn, *Jewish Music: Its Historical Development* (New York: Dover Publications, 1992).

Alan Levy, *The Bluebird of Happiness: The Memoirs of Jan Peerce* (New York: Harper Collins, 1976).

Sara Pendergast (author, editor) and Tom Pendergast (editor), *St. James Encyclopedia of Popular Culture* (Farmington Hills, MI: Gale Publishing Group, 1999).

S. Rosenblatt, *Yossele Rosenblatt: The Story of His Life* (New York: Farrar, Straus and Young, 1954).

Robert Rothstein, "Songs & Songwriters" YIVO Encyclopedia, http://www.yivoencyclopedia .org/article.aspx/Songs_and_Songwriters.

Nahma Sandrow, *Vagabond Stars: A World History of Yiddish Theater* (New York: Harper & Row, 1977).

Henry Sapoznik, Sam Weiss, CD liner notes, *Mysteries of the Sabbath: Classic Cantorial Recordings 1907–47* (Yahoo, 1995).

Marc Slobin, ed., *Old Jewish Folk Music: The Collections and Writings of Moshe Beregovski* (Philadelphia: University of Pennsylvania Press, 1982).

Yale Strom, *The Book of Klezmer: The History, the Music, the Folklore, from the 14th Century to the 21st* (Chicago: A Cappella Books, 2002).

NOTES

1. "Development of Yiddish Over the Ages: Yiddish Dialects," JewishGen.org, http://www.jewishgen.org/databases/givennames/yiddial.htm (accessed September 7, 2011).

2. Abraham Z. Idelsohn, *Jewish Music: Its Historical Development* (New York: Dover Publications, 1992), 17.

3. Ibid., 18.

4. Ibid., 20.

5. Yale Strom, *The Book of Klezmer: The History, the Music, the Folklore, from the 14th Century to the 21st* (Chicago: A Cappella Books, 2002), 4, n10.

6. Judith Kaplan Eisenstein, *Heritage of Music: The Music of the Jewish People* (New York: Union of American Hebrew Congregations, 1972), 43.

7. S. Rosenblatt, *Yossele Rosenblatt: The Story of His Life* (New York: Farrar, Straus and Young, 1954).

8. Alan Levy, *The Bluebird of Happiness: The Memoirs of Jan Peerce* (New York: Harper Collins, 1976).

9. James A. Drake, *Richard Tucker, A Biography* (New York: Dutton Adult, 1984).

10. Henry Sapoznik, Sam Weiss, CD liner notes, *Mysteries of the Sabbath: Classic Cantorial Recordings 1907–47* (Yahoo, 1995).

11. Strom*, The Book of Klezmer*, 30.

12. Robert Rothstein, "Songs & Songwriters," YIVO Encyclopedia, http://www.yivoency clopedia.org/article.aspx/Songs_and_Songwriters (accessed May 9, 2011).

13. Nahma Sandrow, *Vagabond Stars: A World History of Yiddish Theater* (New York: Harper & Row, 1977), 36–39.

14. Strom*, The Book of Klezmer*, 101.

15. Marc Slobin, ed., *Old Jewish Folk Music: The Collections and Writings of Moshe Beregovski* (Philadelphia: University of Pennsylvania Press, 1982), 539.

16. Robert Garfias, "The Romanian Doina," Passion Discs, http://www.passiondiscs .co.uk/articles/doina.htm (accessed February 4, 2010).

17. Sara Pendergast (author, editor), Tom Pendergast (editor), *St. James Encyclopedia of Popular Culture* (Farmington Hills, MI: Gale Publishing Group, 1999).

18. Strom*, The Book of Klezmer*, 5.

19. Idelsohn, *Jewish Music: Its Historical Development,* 380.

Glossary

These are all Yiddish words (many from Hebrew), unless otherwise identified.

Adonoy-Molokh: the Lord is King (name of a klezmer mode)

Ahava Raba: a great love (name of a klezmer mode)

Bar Mitsve: religious ceremony whereby a thirteen-year-old boy becomes a young adult in the Jewish community

Batkhn: wedding bard or jester

Batkhones: witty rhyming songs sung by the batkhn

Baveynen di kale: the lamenting of the bride

Bazetsn di kale: the seating of the bride

Bratsche: viola or second violin

Bulgarish: an up-tempo dance

Dobranots: good-night dance (Polish)

Dobranotsh: good-night dance (Russian)

Doyne: a display piece that is semi-improvised

Dreydlekh: klezmer ornamentations

Dudelzack: German version of the French bagpipe called a *musettet* (German)

Dulce Melos: a kind of hammer dulcimer (Italian)

Dveykes: religious ecstasy

Fantazi: nondance tune often played at the wedding table to honor newlyweds

Freylekhs: most common upbeat klezmer dance

Gezegn: a farewell melody played while walking people home after the wedding

Glitshn: a glissando note in klezmer music ornamentation

Guimbard: a Jew's harp (French)

Gute nakht tants: a good-night dance

Hackbrett: a kind of hammer dulcimer (commonly used in Austria and Bavaria today, German)

Hakbreydl: a kind of *tsimbl*

Hasapiko: a Greek folk dance

Holzharmonika: a kind of xylophone (German)

Hora: Romanian Jewish dance

Jongleurs: itinerant musicians (French)

Judenharfe: Jew's harp

Judenleier: Jewish hurdy-gurdy

Juden Shpielhaus: Jewish concert/dance hall

Kapelmayster: leader of the band

Kapotes: caftan

Ketsev tants: butcher dance

Kharpe-Shpilers: literally shameful players, musicians who played the Jew's harp or
    guimbard

Khasidim: followers of the Kabbalistic and spiritual philosophy started by Ba'al Shem
    Tov in Poland in the eighteenth century

Khazoke: the claim to, the right, the tenure

Khusidl: a dance similar to the freylekhs often danced by the Khasidim

Khupe tants: a dance by the wedding canopy

Klezmer: Jewish folk musician

Klezmer loshn: the klezmer's argot

Kneytshn: short squeezed note in klezmer music ornamentation

Kolomeyke: Carpathian circle dance

Koyletch tants: a dance with a special large egg bread at Jewish weddings and certain
    Jewish holidays

Kozatshok: a Ukrainian Cossack dance

Krekhtsn: moaning long notes in klezmer music ornamentation

Kvetshn: squeezed notes in klezmer music ornamentation

Lancer: a Jewish folk dance

Lautare: folk musician (Romanian)

Letsim: clowns, jesters, buffoons

Marshalik: wedding jester or master of ceremonies

Mazl Tova tants: congratulations dance

Mazurka: up-tempo Polish dance

Minnesingers: the German troubadours of the twelfth to fourteenth centuries

Mishebeyrakh: he who blesses (a klezmer mode)

Misnagdic: an orthodox opponent to the Khasidim

Mitsve tants: good-deed dance

Mogen-Avos: the guardian of our fathers (a klezmer mode)

Moralne: a morality display tune played at a wedding or pre-Yom Kippur

Musetett: a French bagpipe

Musikant: musician

Narim: fools, clowns

Nigunim: generally wordless melodies often sung by the Khasidim

Onge: a Bessarabian line-dance in 2/4 time (sometimes hora) (Romanian)

Ov-Horakhamim: father of mercy (a klezmer mode)

Padekater: a dance piece in 12/8 time

Padespan: a Russian waltz based upon Spanish themes

Payes: earlocks

Polka: an up-tempo Bohemian dance in 2/4

Positive: a fixed organ common in sacred and secular music particularly during the Renaissance and Baroque periods

Portative: a portable small organ common in secular music for the twelfth to sixteenth centuries

Possenreiser: jester, buffoon (German)

Purimshpilers: actors in a play commemorating Haman's defeat, performed on Purim

Rebe: a spiritual leader of a particular Khasidic sect

Sanhedrin: an assembly of twenty-three judges appointed in every city in ancient Israel

Sekund: second violin, viola

Sher: a klezmer square dance with couples

Shpielleutter: itinerant musicians (German)

Shpilman: an intinerant musician

Shteygers: musical mode similar to a scale

Sirba: a Romanian circle or couple dance

Skotshne: a hopping dance or sometimes an instrumental display piece (Polish)

Stroyfidl: a kind of straw xylophone

Taksim: a slow display piece that uses improvisation mixed with *fioratura*

Talis: a prayer shawl

Terkisher gebet: a Romanian display piece with Turkish musical influences

Tish nigunim: table songs, often wordless, sung by the Khasidim around the Sabbath table

Tshoks: bent notes in klezmer ornamentation

Tsimbl: a hammer dulcimer

Tsitsis: the tassels on the *talis* or undergarment worn by Orthodox Jews; also the garment itself

Volekh: a semi-improvised piece similar to a doyne. Could also be an up-tempo melody similar to a freylekhs

Yenuka: baby

Yom Kippur: the day of atonement, the holiest Jewish holiday

Zay Gezunt: a farewell dance played for the newlyweds and their families as they walked home after the wedding celebration

Zhok: a Romanian klezmer dance piece in 3/8, sometimes played for the wedding party as they walked in the street

Zink: cornet or cornetto played during the Renaissance

Zinkennistern: cornetists

Zogckhts: a plaintive display piece

Bibliography

Adler, Henry, and Glickman, Henry F. *Buddy Rich's Modern Interpretation of Snare Drum Rudiments*. Amsco Publications, 1942.

Aldridge, John. *Guide to Vintage Drums*. Centerstream Publications, 1994.

Beregovskii, Moises. *Folkslider: Naye Materyan Zamlung*. Edited by Z. Skuditski. Moscow: Emes, 1933.

Bick, Moshe. *Khatunot Yehudit: Niginot v'Zikhronot*. Haifa, Israel: Haifa Music Museum and AMLI Library, 1964.

Cohen, Bob. "Jewish Music in Romania," 2000–2009. http://www.klezmershack.com/articles/1972.moldavia.shvarts.html.

Dawidowicz, Lucy S. *The Golden Tradition: Jewish Life and Thought in Eastern Europe*. Boston: Beacon Press, 1967.

Drake, James A. *Richard Tucker, A Biography*. New York: Dutton Adult, 1984.

Eisenstein, Judith Kaplan. *Heritage of Music: The Music of the Jewish People*. New York: Union of American Hebrew Congregations, 1972.

Fater, Issacher. *Yidishe Muzik in Poyln Tsvishn Beyde Velt- Milkhomes*. Tel Aviv: Velt Federatsia fun Poylisher Yidn, 1970.

Hart, Mickey, Lieberman, Fredric, and Sonneborn, D.A. *Planet Drum: A Celebration of Percussion and Rhythm*. Acid Test Production, 1998.

Horowitz, Joshua. "The Klezmer Accordion." 2001. www.budowitz.com.

Idelsohn, Abraham Z. *Jewish Music: Its Historical Development*. New York: Dover Publications, 1992.

Kremenliev, Boris A. *Bulgarian-Macedonian Folk Music*. Berkeley: University of California Press, 1952.

Lang, Phillip J. *Scoring for the Band*. New York: Mills Music Inc.,1950.

Levy, Alan. *The Bluebird of Happiness: The Memoirs of Jan Peerce*. New York: Harper Collins, 1976.

Nettl, Paul. *Alte jüdische Shpielleute und Musiker*. Prague: Dr. J. Flesch, 1923.

Ottens, Rita, and Rubins, Joel. *Klezmer-Musik*. Munich: Barenreiter, 1999.

Reck, David. *Music of the Whole Earth*. New York: Da Capo Press, 1997.

Rivkind, Isaac. *Klezmorim: Perek b'Toldotha'Amanot ha'Amamit*. New York: Futuro Press Inc., 1960.

Rosenblatt, S. *Yossele Rosenblatt: The Story of His Life*. New York: Farrar, Straus and Young, 1954.

Rothstein, Robert. "Songs & Songwriters." YIVO Encyclopedia. www.yivoencyclopedia.org/article.aspx/Songs_and_Songwriters.

Saculet, Emil. *Yidishe Folks-Lider*. Bucharest: Editura Muzicala, 1959.

Sandrow, Nahma. *Vagabond Stars: A World History of Yiddish Theater*. New York: Harper & Row, 1977.

Sapoznik, Henry, and Weiss Sam. CD liner notes. *Mysteries of the Sabbath: Classic Cantorial Recordings 1907–47*. Yahoo, 1995.

Slobin, Mark. Ed. and trans. *Old Jewish Folk Music: The Collections and Writings of Moshe Beregovski*. Philadelphia: University of Pennsylvania Press, 1982.

Strom, Yale. *Dave Tarras: The King of Klezmer*. Edited and written by Yale Strom. Kfar Sava, Israel: Or-Tav Music Publications, 2010.

Strom, Yale. *The Book of Klezmer: The History, the Music, the Folklore—From the 14th Century to the 21st*. Chicago: A Cappella Books, 2002.

Svart, Itsik Kara. *Yungen Yornun . . . Veyniker Yunge*. Bucharest: Editura Kriterion, 1980.

Tkachenko, Paul. "Klezmer Bass: An Overview." 2009. www.tkachenko.co.uk/introtoklezmerbasspaultkachenko.pdf.

Index

Note: Page numbers in *italics* refer to figures and tables.

Contributors

David Licht (percussionist) was born in Detroit where he studied piano with his cousin Rene Cash at ages seven through nine. His first images of the drum kit were realized just before moving to Greensboro, North Carolina, in 1965, at age eleven. He studied rudimentary and jazz drumming with Sam Anflick through age thirteen when he purchased his first set. Licht played in rock and jazz bands through high school and played big band jazz at the University of North Carolina at Greensboro, where he studied biology and art on a path to become a medical illustrator. In 1978 he studied at the Creative Music Studio in Woodstock, New York, where he met guitar wild man Eugene Chadbourne. They toured and recorded along with keyboardist/producer Kramer as the band Shockabilly from 1980–1985. Moving to New York City after the band imploded, Licht met Frank London and became a founding member of the Klezmatics, which is still active today. In 1985 Kramer and Licht along with singer performance artist Ann Magnuson and several guitar players toured and recorded as the band Bongwater, which also imploded after five years. After twenty years of touring with the Klezmatics, Licht took a sabbatical and decided to go part-time to focus on raising his family. He is a painter and plasterer in the New York City area and still performs and tours on occasion. Licht met Yale Strom in Krakow and realized on the way to their first gig together in New York that they had lived two blocks from each other back in Detroit in the 1960s and actually had the same art teacher in fourth grade.

Jeff Pekarek (bass) began playing trumpet and guitar at age ten. By age twelve he was familiar enough with the piano to begin learning the art of arranging from his grandfather (a U.S. Navy bandleader). Jeff discovered the double bass at fourteen and made it his life's work. He became a contracted member of the San Diego Symphony at seventeen, performing with the orchestra from 1975–1979. In 1981 he became an independent bandleader, fronting several period music and folk music ensembles.

In 1988 he founded The Electrocarpathians, a band dedicated to fusing vintage rock and classic Latin sounds with East European folk music. In 1996 he began to focus on working as a freelance bassist and has recorded extensively since then with various bands in San Diego, including Keltik Kharma and the Peter Pupping Quartet. He is also the principal arranger for filmmaker and composer Yale Strom, a collaboration that includes two documentary films, numerous chamber works, two ballets, and the orchestral work "Aliyot," performed by the St. Louis Symphony. Jeff is the bassist on bluegrass legend Richard Greene's most recent album, *Shufflin'*. From 2004 to 2008, he worked as an arranger for Canum Entertainment. In 2006 he was the bassist for the theatrical documentary *Primal Twang*, backing up Dan Crary, Eric Johnson, Albert Lee, Mason Williams, and other major artists. Today Jeff continues to work as an arranger, bassist, and audio editor. See www.alterationsgarden.com/jeff_pekarek.htm.

Elizabeth Schwartz (vocals) is celebrated for her uniquely dusky timbre. Multiple reviews hail her "soulful," "passionate," and "penetrating" vocals. She has drawn numerous comparisons to both Edith Piaf and Maria Tanase. From her many appearances with Yale Strom & Hot Pstromi and as a solo artist, Schwartz has built a loyal following among fans, critics, and collaborators. In a historic, barrier-breaking concert, Schwartz was the first woman ever to sing in New York City's 125-year-old landmark Eldridge Street Synagogue. She performs regularly across North America and Central, Eastern, and Northern Europe in venues ranging from jazz clubs to concert halls, as well as synagogues (Schwartz has performed in the two largest synagogues in Europe, in Budapest and Strasbourg) and festivals. She regularly performs with Yale Strom, Alicia Svigals, Mark Dresser, Salman Ahmad, and Samir Chatterjee and has recorded and concertized with many others, including Hungarian supergroup Muzsikas, *tsimbl* maestro Kalman Balogh, Romanian panflutist Damian Draghici, guitar legend Lulo Reinhardt, Marta Sebestyen, fiddle legend Mark O'Connor, Andy Statman, and others. Schwartz also performs with the Common Chords ensemble, which explores harmony, peace, understanding, improvisation, and great music between traditionally conflicted cultures. Schwartz is the subject of the documentary film, *Rumenye, Rumenye: Searching for Schwartz*, directed by acclaimed Romanian filmmaker Radu Gabrea. Schwartz's first recording of Yiddish, Hebrew, and Ladino vocals for the Naxos World label, "Garden of Yidn," debuted on Canada's Mundial Top World Music poll. It was hailed as "a landmark in modern Yiddish song" (*Sing Out!* magazine). Her vocals can be heard on the sound track for the documentary film *L'Chayim, Comrade Stalin!*, as well as on the acclaimed Naxos World releases "Garden of Yidn" and " Café Jew Zoo"; "Dveykes (Adhesion)," with Yale Strom, Marty Ehrlich, Mark Dresser, Diane Moser, and Benny Koonyevsky (Global Village Music); "The Absolutely Complete Klezmer II" (Transcontinental); "Borsht with Bread, Brothers"; and "The Devil's Brides" (both with ARC Music UK). Schwartz is also a writer and an independent filmmaker and former Hollywood film executive. She produced and wrote the documentary films *L'Chayim, Comrade Stalin!* and *Klezmer on Fish Street*.

With Strom, she coauthored *A Wandering Feast: A Journey through the Jewish Culture of Eastern Europe* (San Francisco: Jossey-Bass, 2005). Also with Strom and coauthor Ellen Kushner, Schwartz created *The Witches of Lublin*, an award-winning one-hour audio drama based on a family of women klezmers in eighteenth-century Poland. Please visit her website, www.voiceofklezmer.com.

Norbert Stachel is a multi-instrumentalist (all woodwinds) recording and performance artist. He has long been recognized for his individualized soloistic style on saxophones, clarinets, and flutes. Norbert has appeared on many recordings, live performances, and concert DVD footage with such great artists as Aerosmith, Tower of Power, Roger Waters, Tony Toni Toné, Clarence "Gatemouth" Brown, Prince, Tito Puente, Diana Ross, Boz Scaggs, Neil Diamond, En Vogue, The Temptations, Sheila E., Quincy Jones, Les McCann, Don Cherry, Freddie Hubbard, Roy Hargrove, Andrew Hill, and many others. His website is www.norbertstachel.com.

Peter Stan (accordionist) is of Balkan Roma decent. His parents moved from Serbia to Melbourne, Australia, where he was born and lived until he was twelve. At an early age his father who was an accordionist began to teach him how to play the instrument. Peter then went on to study further with Matthew Aldini (Queensboro Institute of Music), Dr. Jacob Nupauer, Stanley Darrow, and Joan Arnold. After his formal studies, Peter continued to learn from other great Balkan Roma accordionists that he studied and played with. Over the years he has won several prestigious prizes in national accordion competitions including those sponsored by the American Accordion Musicological Society and the Long Island Music Teachers Association.

Besides playing Balkan music, Peter has played a wide variety of genres, with different ensembles that have taken him to many nationally and internationally known venues. Some of these venues and ensembles are: Carnegie Hall, Merkin Hall, International Accordion Festival in San Antonio, Sirius String Quartet (Gregor Huebener), Off Broadway, Mayim Mayim Project in Fuerth in Germany, Montreal Jazz Festival, New Orleans Jazz Festival, Mark Morris dance group, toured in the United States with the legendary Roma vocalist Saban Bajramovic, accompanied famous Balkan singers from Serbia, and toured in Hong Kong, Germany, France, Switzerland, Denmark, Sweden, Turkey, Serbia, South Africa, and Zimbabwe. He is a member of Yale Strom & Hot Pstromi and of Slavic Soul Party. Visit his website, www.peterstanaccordion.com.

Yale Strom (violinist) is one of world's leading ethnographer-artists of klezmer and Roma music and history. Strom's klezmer research was instrumental in forming the repertoire of his klezmer band, Hot Pstromi, based in New York and San Diego. Since organizing his band in 1981, he has composed original New Jewish music that combines klezmer with Khasidic melodies, as well as Rom, jazz, classical, Balkan, Arabic, and Sephardic motifs. Strom's compositions range from a violin solo to string quartets to a full symphony. These works have been performed by Rachel Barton

Pine, Mike Block, the St. Louis Symphony Orchestra, San Diego Chamber Orchestra, Hausmann Quartet, Bordeaux String Quartet, and the Ostrava Philharmonic of the Czech Republic. He has composed original music for several productions of Tony Kushner's *The Dybbuk* as well as all the original music for the National Public Radio series, *Fiddlers, Philosophers & Fools: Jewish Short Stories from the Old World to the New*, hosted by Leonard Nimoy. In addition, Strom has composed music for The History Channel, ESPN, and countless other TV offerings. Yale's thirteen CDs run the gamut from traditional klezmer to "new" Jewish jazz. His CDs (*Café Jew Zoo*, Naxos; *Borsht with Bread, Brothers*; ARC UK, *Absolute Klezmer*, Vol. 1, Transcontinental Music; *Absolute Klezmer*, Vol. 2, Transcontinental Music) have received major rave reviews and been featured on Top Ten Album of the Year lists. His newest CD is *The Devil's Brides* (2011) on the ARC UK label and has the British actress Miriam Margolyes narrating the liner notes. In 2006 he was appointed artist-in-residence in the Jewish Studies program at San Diego State University. Prior to this appointment, Strom taught for many years at New York University.

As a collaborator, Strom has had numerous world-renowned partners, including Andy Statman, Mark Dresser, Marty Ehrlich, Mark O'Connor, Alicia Svigals, Joel Rubin, Hankus Netsky, Peter Sprague, Mike Block, Samir Chatterjee, Salman Ahmad, Gavin Rossendale, Damian Draghici, and Kalman Balogh, to name but a few. With Salman Ahmad, Strom is cofounder of the world music ensemble Common Chords and together performed at the United Nations General Assembly in the recent "Concert for Pakistan." He is also the first klezmer violinist to be invited to instruct master classes at the Mark O'Connor Fiddle Camps.

Strom has also directed eight award-winning ethnographic documentary films (some of which are about klezmer), has exhibited his photos around the world, (some are in private museum collections), and has written two plays and cowrote the radio drama *The Witches of Lublin* costarring Tovah Feldshue, Simon Jones, and Neil Gaiman.

Strom was the guest curator for the Eldridge Street Project's "A Great Day on Eldridge Street." Strom conceived this idea for a musical and photographic celebration of the newly restored landmarked Eldridge Street Synagogue in October 12–14, 2007, with a parade, a historic archival photo shoot, numerous panels and performances, and a New York statewide tour. The historic photo is now available as a poster from the Eldridge Street Synagogue in New York City.

Strom is a dedicated educator and has lectured extensively all over the world. His lectures and concerts at schools across the United States have ranged from how kids can use art to further their understanding of their ever changing world, to an examination of how music can be used to reach across various cultural, ethnic, racial, and religious divides, and how to be a professional artist.

Strom's work as an author includes *The Book of Klezmer: The History, the Music, the Folklore* (Chicago: Chicago Review Press, 2002), a four-hundred-page history with original photos and sheet music gathered by Strom during his sixty-plus ethnographic trips to Central and Eastern Europe; and *A Wandering Feast: A Journey through the*

Jewish Culture of Eastern Europe, written in collaboration with his wife, Elizabeth Schwartz, it is part cookbook, part travelogue (San Francisco: Jossey-Bass, 2005). He is also the author of *The Absolutely Complete Klezmer Songbook* (New York: URJ Press, 2006). His Young Adult books: *Uncertain Roads: Searching for the Gypsies* and *Quilted Landscapes: Immigrant Youth in America Today* have been critically used in schools throughout America. His first illustrated children's book, *The Wedding That Saved a Town* (Minneapolis: Kar-Ben, 2008) won the Best Children's Illustrated Book award from the San Diego Library Association. His most recent book is *Dave Tarras: The King of Klezmer* (Kfar Sava, Israel: Or-Tav Music Publishers, 2010), which is the first biography on the iconic klezmer clarinetist. His website is www.yalestrom.com.